The Simple Path to Amazon Wealth

ISBN: 978-1-7371284-0-3 (Paperback)
ISBN: 978-1-7371284-1-0 (Kindle)

THE SIMPLE PATH TO AMAZON WEALTH

Tom Wang

Contents

Preface

Let me tell you what this book isn't about.

This isn't a get-rich-quick book. This isn't a self-help book. And this isn't about me making money from selling books, either.

Trust me.

I'm always open to new ways of earning money. But there is no money in books. So I'm not going to make money by selling you books.

I've sold my business for multiple 7-figures.

If all I did was leave the cash I have in savings, I would have enough money to retire if I wanted to.

One of the reasons I'm doing this is because I truly love business.

I love talking about business. I love creating businesses. And I love sharing and documenting my journey of creating businesses.

This book is just one of the many ways I'm expressing this.

Also, in the times we live in, I believe that everybody can make a great living online—especially in e-commerce.

With enough dedication, motivation, and the right information, there is truly not a single person who can't eventually find at least some small level of success.

With the rest of this book, you'll see why so many people eventually choose to sell products on Amazon. And exactly what to do to get started.

You'll understand why I get so much joy in sharing my journey too.

Just by sharing what you're about to see, I've been able to change the lives of a lot of my closest friends and others who were in the same depressing situations I used to be stuck in.

Take, for example, my best friend since high school, Dan Kogan.

If I can help you do a fraction of what he was able to do in his first year on Amazon—I know the business opportunities we can create together would be endless.

In 2019, my best friend, Dan, was fired from his job. No heads up. No real reason. And just like that, he lost his only source of income and his entire direction in life.

Having worked for this company for years, Dan couldn't help but feel betrayed.

He had devoted himself to his job. But the only work experience he had was in the car industry.

So once he lost his job, now what can he do?

Sure, he could've searched for a new job, but would that have solved his problem?

In the end, Dan realized that having a job means only having one source of income. If you lose your job, you lose your entire income. In other words, you are 100% reliant on your company to earn a living. That's what some people would call a corporate slave.

Dan didn't want to fall back into another job where he had no control over his life, so he searched for other options. As it turned out, he had a friend (me) who had been egging him on to start selling products on Amazon for years.

You see, I started selling on Amazon in 2017. It wasn't a smooth path to success as you'll see later in this book, but by October of 2018, I surpassed $1,000,000 in revenue for the first time. Sure, it wasn't all profit, but that number caught Dan's eye.

Finally, I got him to say: "Okay, I'm going to do this."

I started showing him my entire system of selling products on Amazon—the exact system you will receive as well. I showed him where I found product opportunities, how I got suppliers, how I was able to get to the top pages of Amazon, and more.

Would you believe it?

Within 8 months, he went from $0 to earning over $100,000 per month in revenue. So he was making about $20,000 to $30,000 a month in profit.

Now, those are some results. Life-changing results!

Dan said, "I'm enjoying my work a lot more because I'm building something real for myself, which is something that I've never had before, and that's the most special part of it all."

He was able to accomplish a lot in such a short period of time. It might even sound unbelievable at first. Some people might say it's because I was there to do the work for him. But really, what I did was just guide him through my mentorship program called FBA Masterclass—and I didn't give him any special attention.

I simply gave him the same level of training I give to the rest of my students.

Actually, that might be a lie. If anything, my mentorship program today is probably more complete and more detailed than anything I showed Dan back in 2019.

That just goes to show, you don't need to be perfect to change your life. You simply have to follow what's been proven to work and take action.

Dan took action and I loved being able to see his transformation. It has to be the best feeling in the world.

That's why I wrote this book. I want to be able to help others thrive in this crazy world.

So if you read till the very end, I'll lay out the entire framework I use for starting a business on Amazon.

Let's get started.

1

THE OLD WORLD VS. THE NEW WORLD

"I felt like I was sleepwalking at my day job."

— Ching

Ching was working in tech for a marketing platform, but she didn't want to be stuck in the same job forever. Now, she's earning over $20,000 per month in revenue online by selling products on Amazon.

Most of us were probably taught to go to school, get good grades, and find a good stable job.

However, the days when it was normal to work with the same company for 40 years are a thing of the past.

Your parents were probably right to teach you the way they did. I mean it worked for them and it's probably worked for you... so far.

But a lot has changed in the world over the past few decades. The same methods that used to work aren't working anymore.

You can thank the internet for this dramatic change. Even just 20 years ago we were living in a completely different world.

We now live in what many experts call the Gig Economy. The gig economy is where more and more companies are moving away from full-time staff with full benefits. Instead, they hire part-time contractors.

The New York Times obtained an internal document that reports Google employing about 121,000 temp workers and contractors in 2019.

According to the International Labor Organization, about 34% of the workforce in the United States in 2017 (or 55 million people) were doing some type of gig work. They said it was projected to rise to 43% as of 2020.

Also, in an Intuit 2020 report, they show that more than 80% of large corporations plan to change their recruitment strategies to hire more 'nontraditional' workers.

In an Upwork study, "Freelancing in America," they found that about 51% of freelancers would choose not to go back to traditional work no matter how much money was offered.

According to a case study by Brodmin and data provided by Mastercard, the global gig economy is expected to be worth almost $350 billion US dollars as of 2021. That's up from $204 billion in 2018 and it's only expected to grow.

With so many statistics pointing to the rise of gig work, and so much competition and new technologies all over the world, is your job really secure?

How do you thrive in this new economy?

Well, I can only give you the answer I know.

You see, back in 2017, I was still working at my old corporate sales job.

I was making good money (about $150,000 a year), but I couldn't imagine myself doing the same old job 10 or 20 years in the future. I tried everything under the sun to try and make it out there on my own.

I made a few dollars here and there, but it wasn't enough to live on. That is until I found one thing...

Amazon.

Within 3 years, I was able to build and sell my business Sdara Skincare for multiple 7-figures. I was able to accumulate over $10M of wealth before I turned 30. I have a 7-figure real estate portfolio, stock portfolio, and crypto along with other investments.

If I choose not to, I don't need to work anymore.

Of course, it wasn't a straight path to success.

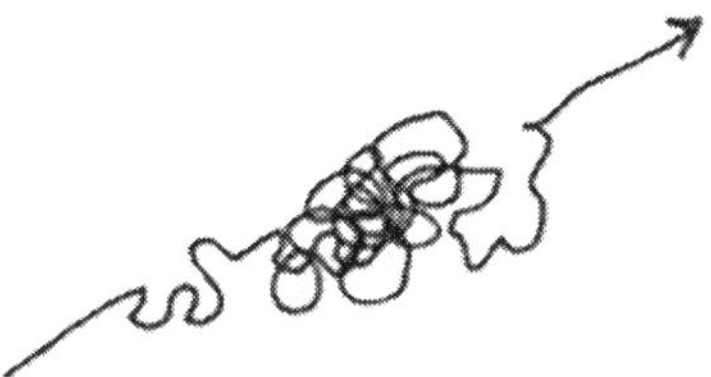

** This is a picture I always show anyone who wants to do any type of business*

There were a lot of ups and downs. But in this book, I want to tell you exactly how I got here and how you might be able to copy-paste some of my results.

First, let me explain how ordinary people are finding massive success online even though they have zero experience.

2

THE GOLDEN ERA OF ECOMMERCE

"The business model is simple. Doesn't mean it's easy, but it's still simple."

—David

David used to work as an aerospace engineer, but wanted to move away from the corporate lifestyle. He knew he wanted to get into e-commerce. That's when he found Amazon. Now, he's making $45,000 a month in sales at home.

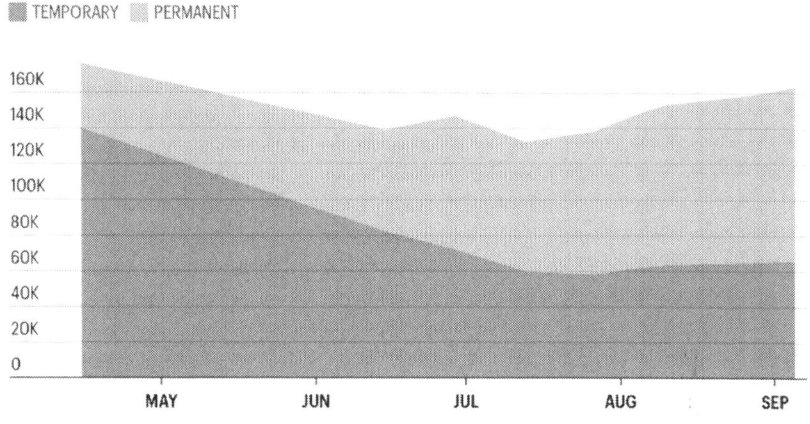

2020 has been hard on a lot of different businesses. More than 100,000 businesses have permanently closed. And these aren't just small mom-and-pop shops that can't keep up with the changes. There are big stores with big names closing too.

This is called the Retail Apocalypse.

It is affecting basically every major retailer you and I grew up knowing.

Here are a few examples:

- JCPenney, which has been around since 1902, filed bankruptcy in 2020 and is expected to close about 30% of the 800+ US stores it had.
- Chuck E. Cheese, founded in 1977, filed bankruptcy in 2020 and has confirmed the permanent closing of 47 centers.
- Guitar Center, founded in 1959, filed for bankruptcy in 2020 with about $1.3 billion in debt.

- Pier 1 Imports, founded in 1962, filed for bankruptcy in 2020 and is closing ALL 991 stores permanently.
- GNC, founded in 1935, filed for bankruptcy in 2020 with more than $1 billion in debt and the plan to close 800 to 1,200 stores.

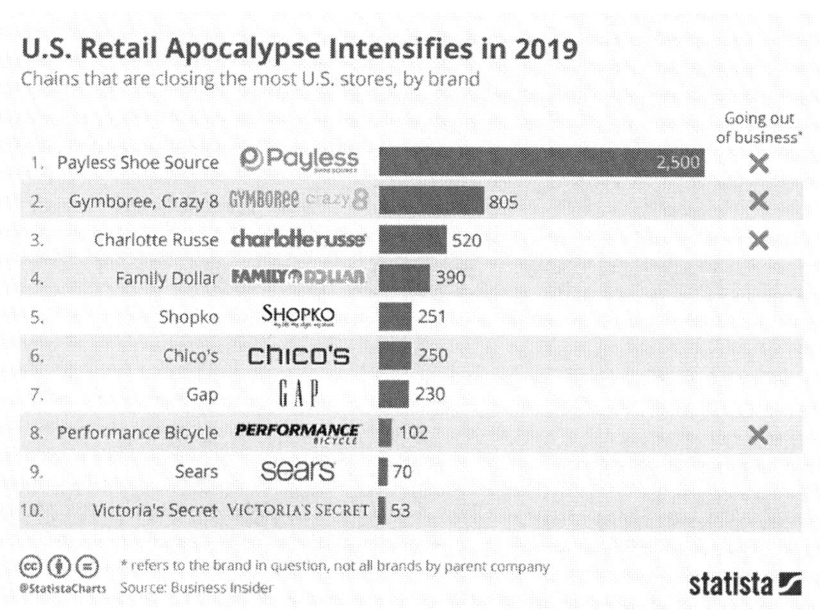

If you haven't noticed, these are not small 'no-name' companies that started yesterday.

These are well-established brands that have made billions. But now they're dropping stores like flies and doing whatever they can to stay afloat.

But What's Happening? Did People Stop Shopping?

You can probably already guess what happened.

I mean, if you wanted to pick up an instrument, would you rather go to Guitar Center and hope to find what you want? Or would you rather browse the internet with an unlimited number of options?

Retail has been on a decline for years. While retail online has exploded.

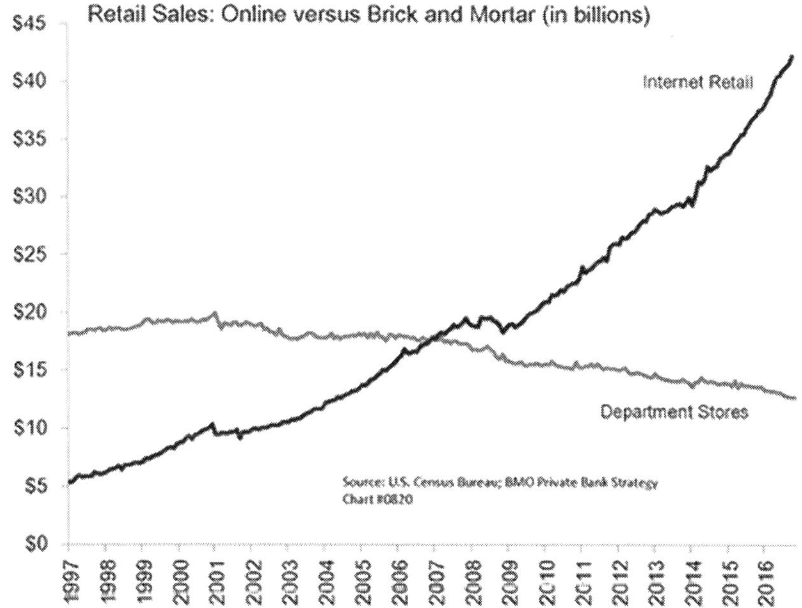

The internet has created a massive shift in behavior.

And because the big corporations don't know how to adapt—you and I can take advantage of this change.

Let's take a look at some examples of people who have been able to find success despite all these stores closing down.

Drunk Elephant — Sold For $845 Million

Tiffany Masterson was just a stay-at-home mom.

She never planned to become an entrepreneur. She even said, "My mom was a stay-at-home mom and had four children, and I really just wanted to do the same thing."

So why did she start Drunk Elephant?

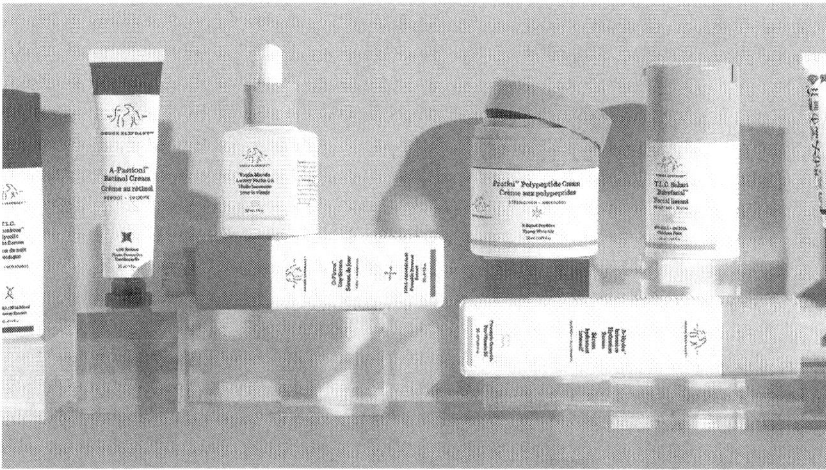

Well, just like any new entrepreneur, she had a problem. For her, it was problems with her skin. As she was doing research, she found 6 problem ingredients that most of the skincare products had—so she decided to make it herself.

She launched the business in 2013. By 2019, the business was doing around $120 million in sales a year and sold for $845 million.

It just goes to show, even stay-at-home moms can become the bread-winners of the family with just a little creativity and a good work ethic.

Native Deodorant — Sold For $100M In 2 Years

Moiz Ali had been using Axe deodorant, but when he was reading the ingredients, he couldn't even pronounce them. His sister ended up saying the same thing about the Dove deodorant she was using.

When you think about it, isn't it weird that we put this stuff on our bodies without even knowing what's in it?

That's when the idea of Native Deodorant came to Moiz. And within 2 years, he was able to sell the company to Procter & Gamble for $100M.

Vessi — Worth 10s Of Millions

Two of my friends, Tony & Mikaella, had some experience selling nano-gloves that allow you to use a smartphone while still wearing the gloves. Through that experience, they had learned a lot about how to market and brand a company.

One day, Tony's friend came to him with an idea for a shoe. He had a prototype and he wanted to raise $30,000. Tony & Mikaella really liked the idea, but they noticed that the positioning could be improved. So they agreed to help and co-launch the company.

They positioned it as "shoes for the rain" and raised $1,260,557 for the first Kickstarter campaign.

They are worth 10s of millions—and growing.

Smart Sweets — Started By A 22-Year-Old And Sold For $360 Million

Tara Bosch loved candy, but she found that it became an unhealthy habit. When she tried to limit sugar from her diet, she ended up craving candy even more. She knew that she should quit eating so much sugar, but the craving was too great.

This is where most people would just give up and continue eating sugar-filled candy anyway. Tara didn't do that. Instead, she experimented with different gummy recipes, which eventually led to SmartSweets.

She created a healthier candy alternative for herself, but she ended up creating a company that sold for $360 million.

MVMT — Founded By College Drop-Outs And Sold For $300M

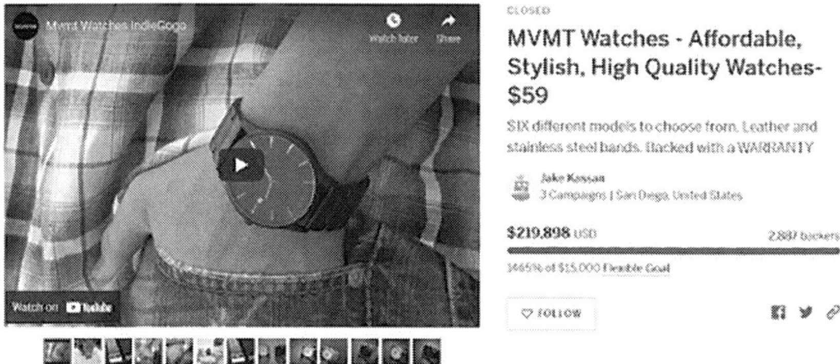

What do you have in mind when you think of a college dropout? A failure? A bum who just likes to party?

Well, Jake Kassan and Kramer LaPlante are college dropouts, yet they were able to raise $291,307 dollars on Indiegogo for a watch. No, not some "high-tech smartwatch." They were just simple watches with a clean design at a reasonable price.

They got the idea because they noticed that most nice watches were very expensive, averaging around $300. But if they went direct-to-consumer, they would be able to cut that price by two-thirds.

With the low price and high-quality design, they were able to take the $291,307 they earned from crowdfunding and built it into a $300 million dollar brand which they sold.

Snow Teeth Whitening — Started By A 20-Something And Worth Over $100M

Josh Elizetxe had started a digital marketing agency when he was 22. It became fairly successful. But there was a time where Josh had to go through jaw surgery and get braces multiple times.

Based on the doctor's recommendation, he had to buy a bunch of different oral products to keep his mouth from going dry. But he didn't like the products. He asked himself, "Why do these products look ugly and medical?"

That piqued his curiosity as he saw an open market for oral care products that didn't feel like you were sitting in the dentist's chair.

After he spoke with his surgeon and dentist, he landed on targeting teeth whitening—which led to Snow Teeth Whitening now being worth over $100 million dollars.

Sdara Skincare — Started By Me, Tom Wang, And Sold For Millions

This is brand I started with my girlfriend at the time (now fiance) in 2017. When I started on Amazon, I knew that I wanted to start a skin-care business. It took me multiple failed attempts to find my winning product—the derma roller.

Early in 2021, Thrasio bought my company for multiple 7-figures. You can now find Sdara on both Amazon and Sdaraskin.com.

Why This Matters To You

As you can see, there are a lot of stories of 20-somethings, single moms, and other ordinary people finding massive success even though most of them had little to zero prior experience.

However, these stories are the height of what is possible.

They even go beyond what I've been able to build for myself. But that's the beauty of getting into this business. You don't have to reach the top to have your life change forever.

But even then, it might be hard to see yourself doing anything similar, even if it is only a fraction of their results. So in the next chapters, I want to share my story from the beginning. That way you can get a clear idea of what it takes to make this happen yourself.

I won't sugarcoat it for you. This is my real journey—the good, the bad, and the ugly.

3

MY LIFE BEFORE SELLING SDARA SKINCARE FOR 7-FIGURES

"Making money out of this business just seemed kind of unreal to me. But it works."

—Jaesung

Jaesung is an international student from South Korea making $10,000 a month while still going to school. He's making more money than some of his professors by selling products on Amazon.

I was able to build and sell Sdara within 3 years of starting.

That seems like a short time, but in reality, I was building up to that moment my entire life.

The first side hustle I still remember was back when I was still living in China. I was in 2nd or 3rd grade at the time. My dad traveled a lot and, when he did, he would bring back pens and pencils that were made in the US.

These items looked very different from those being manufactured in China. So I took the pens and pencils and sold them to my classmates. I would use the money I earned to buy candy and stuff like that. I thought that was pretty cool as a kid.

Later, I immigrated with my family to Canada, which set me on a course that would change my life forever.

Hacking The System

When I was about 15, I used to go up to Grouse Mountain and Whistler Blackcomb a lot and snowboard. So I used to go online and find a bunch of discount deals for snowboarding gear.

That's when I thought, "What if I bought the gear at massive discounts, then sold it on eBay or Craigslist at the normal price?"

So I started buying a bunch of snowboarding gear. Sometimes I'd wear it myself a few times before I sold it. I felt like I was hacking the system.

Flipping Tickets

Whenever a big DJ came into town, I'd buy the tickets and sell them on Craigslist. Basically, I was a scalper.

If I couldn't get rid of the tickets online, then I'd go to the venue myself and sell them right in front of the door.

Making Money Out Of My Parents Home

Back when I lived with my parents I also had an Airbnb business. Yes... I Airbnb'd my parents' home. And I'll tell you, I got an earful when they found out.

My parents were gone for pretty much an entire summer one year. So I rented a room out to a lady and her daughter from Japan. It was one way that I was able to pay my way through college.

Bitcoin Broker

Back when Bitcoin was first gaining popularity, there were a lot of people looking to buy that didn't really know how. That's when I had the idea to act as a broker with these deals.

They gave me their money to buy bitcoin and in exchange I took a transaction fee.

Tangerine Seller

There was this affiliate program I did back in 2013 with a local bank called Tangerine. With their affiliate program, if you refer people to sign up both of you get a hundred dollars. The more people you sign up, the higher the commission you get paid.

I thought it was a good opportunity. So I tried to get as many people to sign up to Tangerine as possible. But let's be honest, it wasn't that great of an opportunity.

I posted ads on Craigslist and my Facebook page and I struggled to gain consistent traffic. I was lucky to make the few thousand dollars that I did.

Selling Blinged-Out Watches

One time, I went to a Vegas trade show to help my dad. There were these massive blinged-out watches. They were like a rapper watch with diamonds around the edges.

The last day of the trade show, I walked up to the vendor and asked them about the watches. It turned out they didn't want to bring them back with them. They just wanted to get rid of them.

That's when I said, "I'll take them." They gave me a good deal and I brought about 50 watches back to Canada with me. I just went down the street and approached anybody I thought would be a good fit for these watches.

I was able to sell them pretty well, so I decided to order more. At that time, one of my friends had a booth at the night market. I asked him to give me some space to sell the watches.

Overall, the mini-business didn't go anywhere, but I was able to make a little bit of money from it.

Exporting Cars To China

One of my friends had gotten into the business of exported cars. He bought cars in Canada and shipped them off to China because people there are willing to pay a lot of money for those cars.

During that time I would help him out. We would buy them outright with cash so we didn't have to finance them. It was a pretty good way to make money. The money I made helped me to go through college.

Fiverr Arbitrage

Fiverr is a great place to make some money on the side, but I didn't do it the way most people do. Most people put their own services on the site and fulfill the job themselves. I didn't really have a lot of skills I could market and make a good income from, so I came up with a different idea.

I bought a bunch of logos, brochures, and business cards. Then I posted them on Craigslist offering those services. If someone placed an order with me, I would just find a guy on Fiverr for $5, $10, or $15 to do the job. Then I would sell the work to make a profit.

Why I Landed On Amazon

I didn't realize it at the time, but I was buying more and more from Amazon. I had no idea that I could sell products on Amazon. For that reason, I didn't think too much about it until one of my friends told me about it.

When I finally started Amazon, I didn't expect to ever make millions. I thought it was going to be a similar story to the rest of the side hustles I did.

Over time, I saw the real potential in Amazon and put all my focus into maximizing results.

But I didn't have a breakthrough immediately after starting Amazon. That was simply step one. In the next chapter, I will take you through the first products I sold on Amazon and what I learned each step of the way.

4

FROM SELLING EXPLODING HOVERBOARDS TO BEAUTY PRODUCTS

"Just do it. If you don't do it - you don't try - you'll never know how you're going to do."

— Hiep

Hiep renovated and constructed houses. He was never much of a tech person so getting into e-commerce was a big leap for him. But he knew that he wanted to get into the Amazon business. He figured it out and is now making over $15,000 a month.

The first product I tried to sell on Amazon quickly blew up. Not in the 'they became very popular sense'—I mean they literally exploded, because the products were faulty.

Remember hoverboards?

Yeah, I thought it would be a smart idea to sell them since they gained a lot of popularity. That was a mistake.

Most of them were defective. I found myself getting down on my knees to fix the hoverboards right in front of the people I was trying to sell them to.

And that wasn't the least of my worries. By the time I actually started selling hoverboards, the fad was already over. Nobody wanted them.

I ended up spending about $5,000 and got nothing in return. I lost a lot of money because I decided to jump into a product that got random popularity.

Even then, I didn't give up. I took the lesson to heart and set out to not make the same mistake. But I may have taken that lesson a little too far.

My First Step Into Beauty Products

If you've spent any time looking at skincare products, you might have come across Vitamin C serum before.

If you don't know what it is, it's meant to brighten skin tone and help reduce the signs of aging.

When I looked it up on Google Trends, it had steady growth. It was popular and people were buying. What more can you ask for?

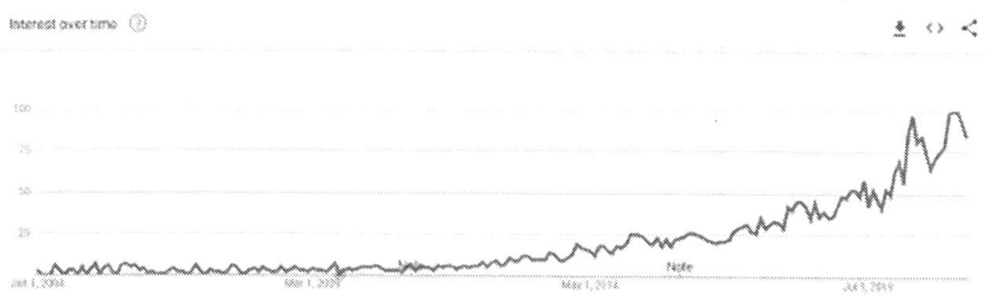

Well, as it turned out, it was TOO popular. There were too many sellers competing for the products. And there were a lot of trusted brands filling that space.

I was able to earn $7,000, but that was short-lived. I ran out of stock very quickly. By the time I got back in stock, it was extremely hard to get ranked again.

I had no idea how the ranking worked. So once I lost it, I started to panic. I did everything I could to try and get the ranking back. I changed the title, the bullet points, the images, everything!

That was my worst mistake. That just messed everything up more. Even if what I did worked, there was no way for me to repeat that success.

I was pretty devastated by that, but I decided to try again.

My Failure That Hurt The Most

I found another product—a makeup sponge. This was a new model that was made out of silicone. Since it was made out of silicone, it was easier to clean and it lasted longer.

At that time, we were thinking that we needed to work on a brand name. I have a friend, Simon, who's a rockstar at branding.

I asked him how much it would cost for his services. It was about $2,500. I didn't have that money. So I asked him if he wanted to partner up on the next product. He's pretty easygoing, so he said yes.

The work he did was incredible. When he showed us the new Sdara branding, I was in awe. It was like a multi-million dollar brand you'd find in a retail store.

So we continued to work to launch our product. He put in 50% of the capital. And I put in the other 50%. It took us a little while to get to market because we wanted to do this one right.

Not only was it gaining attention online, but it was still new enough to not have competition. It seemed like a dream product.

But there was one problem... the product sucked.

I even had some of my female coworkers try it and they all hated it. But I launched the product anyway.

Out of all my failures, that was the one that hurt the most. I was about ready to quit.

That was the breaking point for me. Not only did I lose my money, but I lost my friend's money too. That moment broke me.

I remember a car ride where I asked Christina, "Should we just quit?"

I was basically seeking her permission. If she said yes, I would've quit right there. That's how close I was to quitting. That's how close I was to never building my business. I would've moved on to something else.

But she said, "No."

That was all I needed to continue going at the time. I realized later how much mindset can make or break your chances of success.

If I was just a little bit weaker in my mindset or hadn't had Christina to support me, I wouldn't be where I am today. I might have stayed the same old me, jumping from side hustle to side hustle, never making any progress.

The Moment That Changed My Life

We came across this product that neither of us had ever heard of. It seemed weird at first. It was a roller with microneedles that you use on your face. And it was gaining popularity fast.

In my mind, it was the silicone makeup sponge all over again. I hesitated for a while because I didn't want to make the same mistake.

Several months passed and it was still growing. If it was a fad, it would've fallen by this time. That's when we knew it wasn't just another fad. This was a legitimate product that people actually wanted.

Within a few months of launching, I was making a steady $200,000 a month from this one product alone.

I really couldn't believe it, but it was real. We found a winner!

It really was a moment that changed my life forever. I knew that I could create my own successful business. Unfortunately, with success comes new problems.

The Day It All Went Away

I remember waking up one day in April. Just like any other day, I checked the sales on my phone, but there was something wrong. The sales were really low.

What happened?

I ran to the computer to see what had happened to our Amazon listing. What I found was different sellers straight-up copying our product. It wasn't only the product. It was everything, all the way down to the packaging.

This type of situation is fairly common. It's usually not a big problem, but this was different. Most of the time, when there's a hijacking, there's only one hijacker. In this case, there were 9 or 10 different hijackers.

And then to make matters worse, they somehow got access to our account, allowing them to change our listings and even the brand name.

They hijacked our listing and started selling counterfeit products. I even bought one of their products to see what they were selling. It was a complete fake. The quality was horrible.

Just because some random hijackers wanted to steal my profits, I went from $200,000 a month to $0 in one night.

Talk about having a panic attack. That was all my income... gone at no fault of my own.

I tried anything I could to get the account back. I submitted two appeals to Amazon. I wish that meant problem solved, but both of them got denied.

I can say that this was the lowest point of my entrepreneurial journey.

Eventually, after contacting anyone we could, we were able to figure out how to get our account back and clean up the mess. That situation left a mark on me.

I learned how easy it is for everything to go away. But I also learned how I can defend myself against it happening again. And I learned that I can weather any storm as long as I don't give up.

I Don't Regret A Thing

Sure, I had a lot of ups and downs, but I love what I was able to build. First, I was able to leave my job after my first year in business. Then it took me two years to grow a reliable, multi-million-dollar-a-year business.

Now, I have control over my life and my finances. I can do whatever I want without having to report to a boss.

I am free.

Here's an image of one of my record months when I had an over-$600K month.

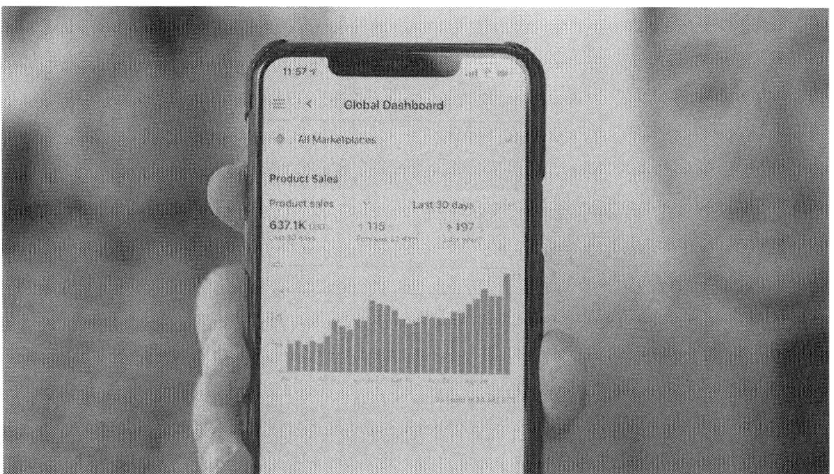

And in December 2020, we officially sold Sdara Skincare to Thrasio (a private company that has bought more than 150 brands on Amazon at the time of writing).

I was able to buy a house in West Vancouver (which is the most expensive real estate in all of Canada).

I was able to buy one of my dream cars, the Audi R8.

And I proposed to my girlfriend Christina. Not to mention, I had absolutely zero worries about financial problems (which is the #2 reason for divorce).

Me proposing to my dream girlfriend at my dream house.

I love life and I only got here because I didn't quit when things got hard.

After hearing my horror stories, there's a chance you might second guess if this is right for you. Don't go too far, because you don't have to struggle the way I did.

I started on my own and had to learn from my own mistakes. You can be different. The reason I share my failures with you is because I know you can learn from them. I want to share what I've learned so you can succeed too.

Like one of my students, JP, said, "It allowed me to skip over mistakes that I would've made if I didn't take the course."

So in the next chapter, I will show exactly why I always recommend new entrepreneurs start with Amazon.

5

ONLINE SALES FOR THE NEWBIE

"There are a lot of things to Amazon that people don't realize. There are so many different areas which you can't really get from just YouTubers or trying to figure it out yourself."

— Hayden

Hayden was a VP of a tech company who was in charge of sales, but he had zero experience with e-commerce. After following a simple system, he was able to start earning $15,000 a month selling products on Amazon.

There is such a huge opportunity on Amazon. Even though I sold Sdara, I'm not backing away from Amazon. I'm doubling down and building/acquiring new Amazon businesses.

And if you're wondering why I chose to continue even though I already had a big payday... here are the real numbers.

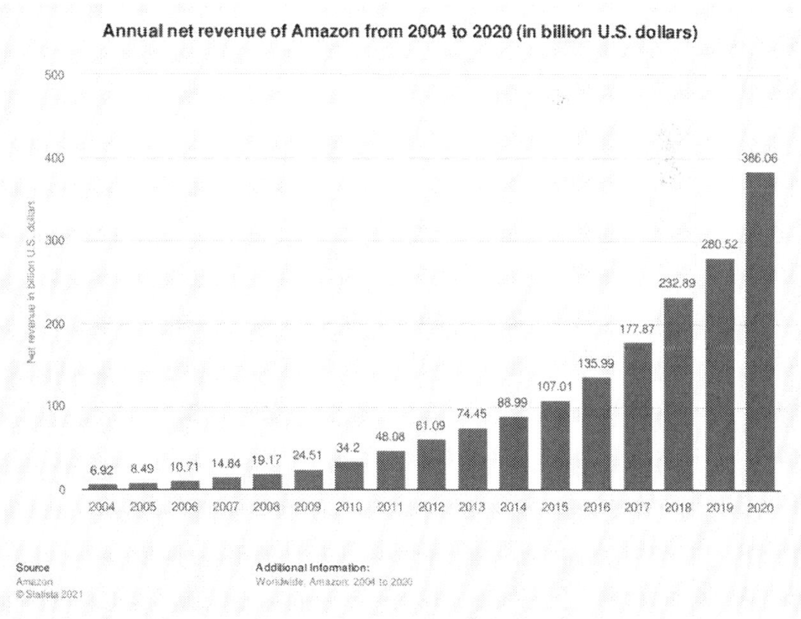

When I found out about Amazon back in 2016, Amazon had about $135 billion in revenue. As you can see, despite having a pandemic throughout 2020, Amazon's revenue has more than doubled within those four years.

At first, you might think, "Is that worth anything to me? Why does Amazon's growth have anything to do with me?"

Well, you see, Amazon doesn't own most of the products it sells. It's more like a massive marketplace. Similar to a mall where there are many different stores owned by many different people.

As a matter of fact, as of 2020, over 55% of all sales on Amazon come from ordinary people like you and me. Amazon calls us "3rd party sellers."

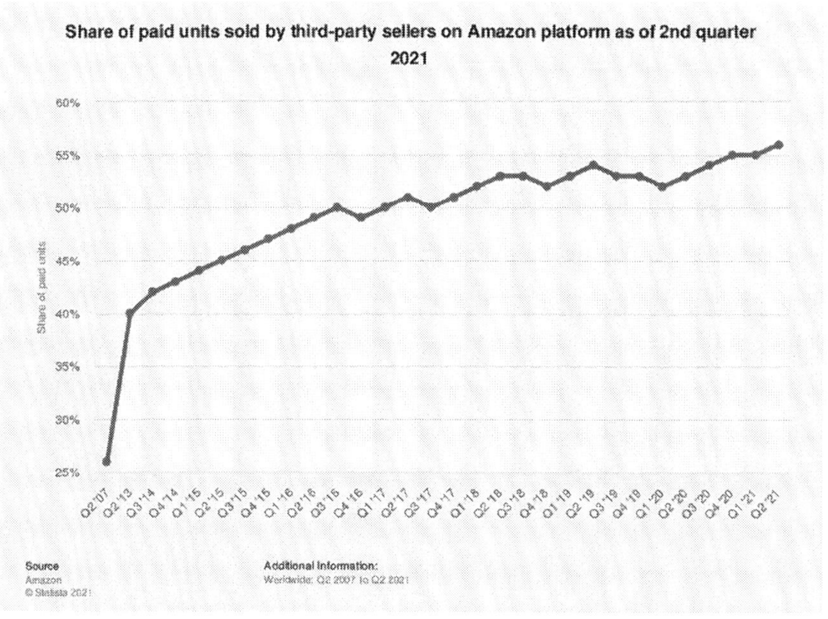

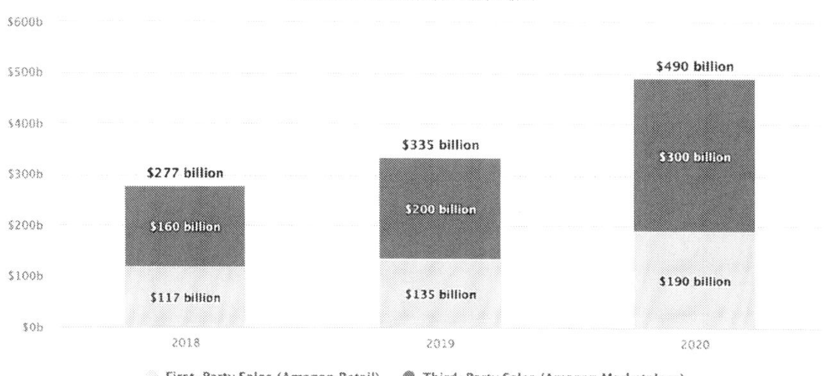

With these numbers alone, every time I hear people saying, "Bitcoin is the next BIG thing! Invest in Bitcoin!" I look at them like they're crazy.

Sure you can make money in Bitcoin, but right now, it's too unstable. It's not something you invest in to make a stable living.

And if you're thinking that selling products on Amazon will take forever to become profitable, then I think you'll be happy to hear this.

It's possible to get your first product on Amazon making a profit in as little as 4 months. That's not an exaggeration.

Imagine being an immigrant from Bangladesh. You're in a completely new environment. You're unfamiliar with the language, so it's a challenge to find good work. For that reason, you struggle to provide the life you want for your family.

It can be hard, taking jobs that you don't really like just so you can pay the bills. Well, this is exactly what happened to Pali.

He couldn't be picky about the job he took, so he found himself living with his head inside refrigerators repairing them.

It's not an exciting job, but it gave him an income to feed his family. But just like any immigrant, he came here with a dream to give his family more. He couldn't do that being a repair guy for the rest of his life. That's when he saw one of my ads talking about Amazon.

It's not like he knew anything about e-commerce or how to sell on Amazon. But he liked what he heard and he took the opportunity.

After following my system, Pali started making over $30,000 a month in sales on Amazon.

These kinds of opportunities on Amazon are real. However, it can seem like these people just got lucky at first.

Even before I started Amazon, I was trying to get into the online space. I wanted to have my own success story, just like all of those incredible stories I shared in the previous chapter. But nothing I did worked.

I even spent $5,000 to build a website and buy supplies... but I got $0 in return. I thought I was out of luck until one of my friends told me about how I could sell the products on Amazon.

I've had the privilege to teach many of my students how to succeed on Amazon. Over and over, I get to see my students achieving real results in a short period of time.

Like Dan, my best friend, who was fired from his car sales job. He knew about what I was doing on Amazon, so he took his job loss as an opportunity.

In just 8 months, he was able to go from $0 to $100,000 a month in revenue.

Or Jennie, who was able to earn a 5-figure-a-month income while working as a nurse during the 2020's pandemic.

There's also David, who went from a normal corporate job to earning $45,000 a month in revenue and working full-time at home.

Not to mention Jaesung, an international student who was able to make $10,000 a month while still going to school.

Then there's Mary, a new mother, who was able to earn $1,000 a day while still on maternity leave.

With all of those success stories of ordinary people getting real, life-changing results, how can you not feel inspired? And there are many more success stories where those came from.

The main reason they're able to get results fast is that they followed my proven system, which took me years to perfect.

The journey isn't always easy. If you want to see what it took for me to get to this winning solution, you can find out in the next chapter.

If you're interested in getting help from a community of 6-8-figure Amazon sellers, then you might want to know more about my mentorship program—FBA Masterclass.

As a student of FBA Masterclass, you receive LIVE group coaching every week, plus over 200+ private training videos that walk you through, step-by-step, what to do on every step of your journey—and more.

To schedule a call to talk to my team, visit
www.fbamasterclass.io/consultation

On your call, my team member will tell you everything you need to know before you decide to start selling on Amazon for yourself, and give you a breakdown of what's included in my mentorship program.

By the end of the call, you might choose to join me and my students in my mentorship program. Or you might choose to go it alone. Either way, the call with my team will give you a good step forward.

6

HOW TO SELL ON AMAZON

"Don't do it yourself because so much information out there is outdated or just super vague."

— Jennie

Jennie started selling on Amazon while working as a nurse during covid. She tried learning on her own for about 4 months and eventually joined my mentorship program. Now, she's making $15,000 a month in sales using the same methods talked about in this chapter.

Selling on Amazon is both an art and a science. The art is in how you set yourself apart from the pack, and the science is in the formula for repeatable success.

This formula has four main action steps:

1. Find a winning product
2. Source your product
3. Launch on Amazon
4. Scale your business

That sounds simple, but there is quite a bit that goes into each of those four steps. The good news is these steps are straightforward and easy to follow. In fact, thousands of my students have made money on Amazon through this very process.

So, let's dive into the meat of it. Here is the step-by-step process of launching your own Amazon FBA business from a high level.

Preface — Solve A Need

Before we jump into the mechanics, I want to discuss what separates successful businesses from unsuccessful ones.

You should not think about this as an Amazon business. This is an eCommerce business that uses Amazon as a platform.

There is Amazon, Shopify, eBay, and Craigslist. Each of these are channels. We use Amazon because it does the heavy lifting for us.

Because this is an e-commerce business, you must understand that you are selling real products to real people. And the number 1 reason why a person wants to buy a product is that they want to solve a specific need in their life.

For example, why do people take weight loss pills? The obvious answer is to lose weight, but if we dig deeper, we discover that people want to feel more confident every day or impress friends and family.

As you are embarking on your e-commerce business and doing your product research, ask yourself, "Does this product solve a specific need in my life or in someone else's life?"

If you can personally relate to the need that it addresses, you already have an understanding for how to innovate on the product and make it better.

But for products that you are not the target user of, you must decide if it's worth becoming an expert on that niche before you start selling it.

To give you a real example, a friend of mine showed me real hair extensions for women. They were doing amazing sales on Amazon, but I know absolutely nothing about what this product solves for.

I'm not a woman. I've never put hair extensions on. I don't know why some of them cost $1,000 and others cost $50. I am not a user, and honestly I don't want to become an expert. So we moved on from that idea.

The next idea we talked through is dog food. I have a Golden Doodle who I love like my own kid. I want to be able to offer him healthy and nutritious food, but kibbles are bad for dogs and air-dried food is too expensive.

I am very familiar with this problem and would feel confident inventing a product around the solution.

So, while I'm going to teach you how to use software to find products, do not rely 100% on these tools alone.

Instead, ask yourself... What are some of the products I use everyday that could be better? As a user of the product, you know the market and you're already on your way to becoming an expert.

This way, if and/or when things get tough, you will still have interest in the problem. Every time I look at my dog, I'm passionate about finding him the right food, and this drive would help me in bringing dog food to market.

To wrap this up, challenge yourself to think about solving a problem and building a better product for real customers on the other side of the digital cart.

Step 1: Find A Winning Product

One of the most important things you can do when starting this business is building it into your routine as a habit. This is a marathon, not a sprint.

So you've got to be committed for the mid-to-long-term. To help with this, I give all of my students access to an FBA Road Map.

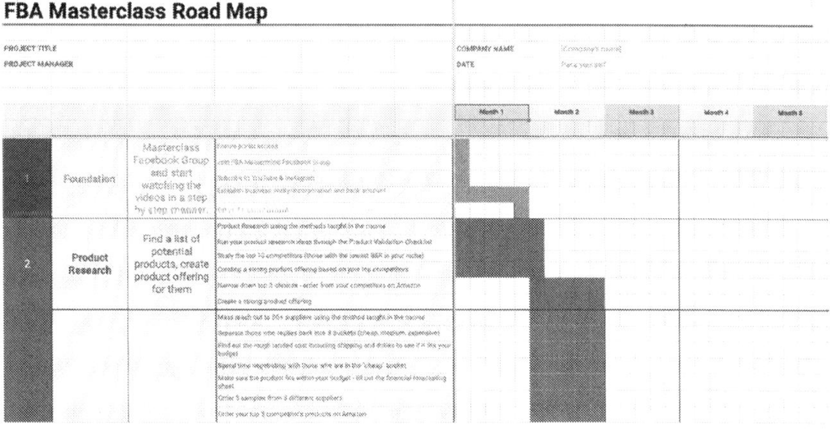

This document is a piece of gold for your Amazon FBA business and will provide you with tons of clarity. You'll see different steps along your FBA journey, along with a "north star" for each stage.

Alright, now that you know where we're headed, here are your very first action steps:

1. *Form a business*: In Canada, form a sole proprietorship or incorporation. In the United States, form an LLC. If you are from other countries, it's best to ask your accountant.

2. *Open a bank account for your small business.* If you are in Canada, I recommend just go into any of the big banks such as RBC, TD, BMO, etc. If you are in the US, check out an online bank called Mercury. They are an online bank with no fees that focuses on helping entrepreneurs. https://www.mercury.com/partner/FBAmasterclass

3. *Apply for an Amazon Seller Central account:* You will need your business information and your bank account to create this.

As laid out in the FBA Road Map, you can begin your product research as you're setting up your business and accounts.

Methods to Find Great Product Ideas

There is not one "right" way to find product ideas. As an example, the founder of GoPro didn't come up with the business through some formula online. Instead, he wanted to capture footage of his surfing adventures in Australia but couldn't find a sturdy enough camera that could withstand the waves. He looked as his own life, found inspiration, and built a great product. So here are 10 methods you can use to come up with product ideas.

Method #1: Scratch your own itch

If you had a magic wand, what are a few things in your day-to-day life that you want to solve for? If these things give you headaches, it's likely they are frustrating for other people too. If you can create a solution for that headache, other people will pay you for it. That's entrepreneurship at its best.

Method #2: Crowdfunding sites

Kickstarter and Indiegogo are great websites to browse through and see which campaigns overperformed and which did not get funded. Many didn't get funded because of execution or operational issues. Use these platforms to get ideas flowing.

Method #3: Read product reviews

On Amazon, eBay, and websites, you can go through customer reviews to find what people are liking (or not liking) about products. If someone says, "I really wish this iPhone case had smoother edges, you can see what already exists and work to improve upon the product to solve customer desires.

Method #4: Taobao

This is a Chinese website that hosts a lot of really cool products. Here, you can browse categories that interest you and find a product that you can bring to the States. Many of the products on Taobao are not yet on Amazon, giving you a first-mover advantage.

Method #5: Etsy

Etsy is a website that features hand-made products. Many of them have amazing designs and come from really passionate creators. See what's hot and selling well to get your creative juices flowing. If a product is selling well on Etsy but isn't yet on Amazon, it can be a great opportunity to carve out your own niche.

Method #6: TikTok

Warning: TikTok can be like crack for your brain. That said, you can use it to find really great product ideas. Download TikTok and search "#amazonfinds" or "#tiktokmademebuythis." You will see a bunch of videos that showcase tons of random, viral, and/or cool products.

Method #7: Exploding Topics

This is a free website that helps you identify rapidly growing topics before they take off. You can either browse the site or sign up for their newsletter, which sends you weekly emerging trends. These trends can serve as inspiration as you're thinking about what to sell.

Method #8: Viral Launch and Helium10

These are software tools designed specifically for Amazon sellers that plug into Amazon and generate product ideas based upon your defined criteria. I must warn you: a lot of people use the same filters, which result in the same product ideas. I'll talk more about how to utilize these tools for validation later, but don't be afraid to generate a wide list of top-level ideas from many different sources.

Method #9: Shark Tank

If you're not watching this show, you definitely should. Every entrepreneur should watch Shark Tank because it gives you amazing ideas and is really motivating, especially when founders make a deal with the sharks. Watch for free online to get those creative juices flowing.

Method #10: Touch Test

This is similar to method #1 in that it centers on solving your daily problems. And... It's my favorite way of finding a million dollar product. If you know something really well, stick to it. Are you a photographer? Innovate on camera gear. Are you a dog owner? Innovate on pet products. As an existing customer, you know what problems exist and how to communicate a solution. It's an instant competitive advantage.

Of course, there is no "perfect" product to sell on Amazon. But there are definitely "bad"

products to launch. And "terrible" ones too. So what makes a "good" one?The first thing to know is that you MUST use data to make this decision. Do not randomly guess which product to sell or go off a gut feeling.

There is lots of data available to Amazon sellers, and with it we can make an informed decision about which products will set us up to make money, and which ones are a disaster waiting to happen.

Some products have insanely high competition. Others don't allow for any profit margin. These are definitely products that you want to stay away from.

At a high level, you want to launch a product with high demand and low competition that will be profitable for the long term. There are software tools designed specifically for Amazon sellers that can help you find these types of products. They give you all the data you need to make a wise decision.

The most popular tools are called Viral Launch and Helium 10 (use code TOMWANG for Viral Launch or code TOMWANG10 for Helium 10 to get a discount).

Now, here's what a good product actually looks like:

Criteria #1: High Demand — There Are Already People Searching For And Buying It.

General rule of thumb: We want to find a product where at least 5,000 people per month are already searching for it on Amazon. We're also looking for a product where three of the top sellers have a Best Seller Rank (or BSR) of less than 20,000, which means multiple existing sellers are already making good money with this product. The lower the BSR, the higher the sales.

Passes The Test: Plant Hanger

If you were shopping for a "plant hanger" on Amazon, these 10 products would pop up in your search results. As an Amazon *seller*, you can use Viral Launch's tool called Market Intelligence to see data about each of these products.

At the top, the tool tells us that the keyword "plant hanger" has an estimated 28,901 searches per month. That surpasses our criteria of 5,000+ monthly searches, which is great. Now if we look at the BSR, I see that *all 10* are below 20,000. That definitely surpasses our criteria. So for high demand, plant hangers get a green checkmark.

Fails The Test: Swim Training Belt

If you're an active swimmer, you may know all the wonderful benefits of swimming with a training belt on. Maybe you're thinking about launching it as your Amazon product. Well, when we dig into the data using Viral Launch's tool called Keyword Research, we see that the monthly search volume for "swim training belt" is 816. That's far below our target of 5,000+. Even the largest associated keyword—"swimming equipment"—only gets 2,818 searches per month. This would be a product to stay away from.

Criteria #2: Low Competition — Top-Selling Products Don't Have A Ton Of Reviews.

General rule of thumb: We want to find a product where the top 10 sellers have less than 400 reviews on average because reviews are tough to acquire as an Amazon seller. This maximum threshold can be higher (around 1,000) if you're able to differentiate your product from the rest of the pack. But as a beginner, it's best to find a market where you can compete quickly with a small number of reviews as you get started.

Passes The Test: Collapsible Stool

Here we've got a product that passes our Search Volume and BSR check from Criteria #1. When we look at the competition, we can see in Market Intelligence that the average page one product has only 270 reviews. That's less than our ideal target of 400, so this product looks to be a winner so far.

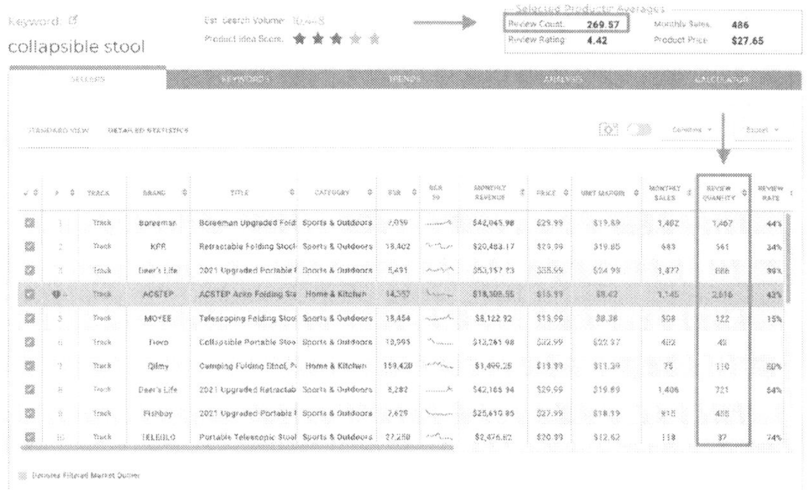

Fails The Test: Toilet Brush

Although this product also passes our High Demand criteria, we can quickly see that there are way too many reviews for a new seller to compete quickly. The average product on page one has 4,832 reviews. This doesn't mean you cannot be successful, but I would advise against a competitive market like this for your very first product.

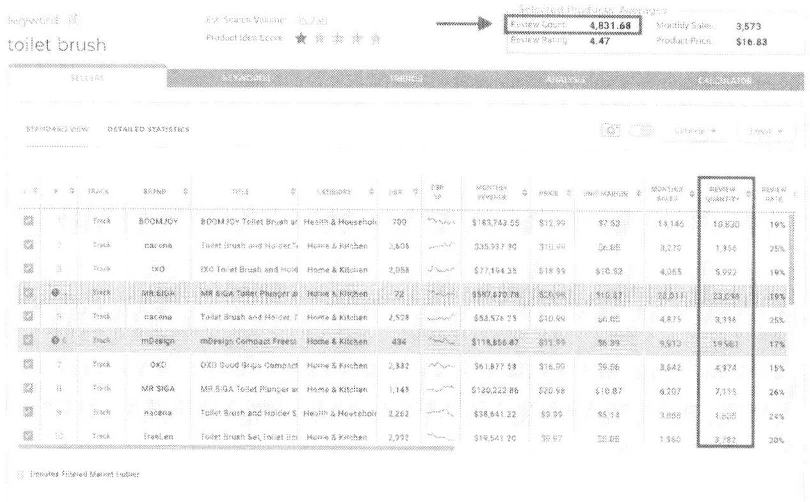

A Quick & Important Note...

This might sound contradictory, but sometimes review count does not matter as much as you may think. You see, when Moiz launched Native Deodorant, there was major competition. Page one results include products with 1,000... 15,000... even 30,000 reviews. Not to mention many of these are by recognizable brands such as Secret, Degree and Dove.

However, Moiz didn't let high reviews stop him. He was able to differentiate the product enough to carve out his own niche. Moiz built a deodorant with a natural spin – aluminum free with probiotics. In this way, the innovation of the product became worth more to shoppers than thousands of reviews on more "harmful" alternatives. And now, Native Deodorant boasts upwards of 60,000 reviews on its most popular SKU. Talk about a powerful product.

Overall Choice

Secret Powder Clean Invisible Solid Antiperspirant and...
2.6 Ounce (Pack of 6)
591
$20.62 ($1.33/Fl Oz)
Save more with Subscribe & Save
prime FREE One-Day

Small Business Brand

Native Deodorant | Natural Deodorant for Women and...
2.65 Ounce (Pack of 1)
64,833
$12.97 ($4.89/Ounce) $15.00 14%
$11.67 with Subscribe & Save discount
prime FREE One-Day

Men's

Dove Men+Care Antiperspirant Deodorant...
2.7 Ounce (Pack of 4)
12,698
$15.66 ($1.45/Ounce) $19.69 20%
$14.88 with Subscribe & Save discount
prime FREE One-Day

The lesson: Reviews do matter, but they should not be the end-all-be-all. While it's important to understand your competition's grasp on the market, you can stand out among the crowd with an innovative product, even with far less reviews. For more information, check out a book called *Blue Ocean Strategy: How to Create Uncontested Market Space and Make Competition Irrelevant* by W. Chan Kim and Renee Mauborgne.

Criteria #3: Profitable — It Fits Your Budget And Makes Money After Expenses.

General rule of thumb: You only want to spend half of your budget on product expenses, so that you have some money left for marketing.

So if you have $5,000 total, you shouldn't spend more than $2,500 on inventory. Additionally, you want to aim for at least a 35% profit margin, so that you have cash flow to reinvest into your business.

Passes The Test: Kids Snorkeling Set

You will need to validate your margin after you get actual quotes from manufacturers. At this initial research stage though, Market Intelligence tells me that kids snorkeling sets are selling on page one for an average of $28. On Alibaba, I see that I should be able to source them for $6. With some estimations on shipping and duties along with fees determined using Amazon's FBA calculator, I predict I can make a 45% profit margin.

Revenue	Price	$28.00
	COGS	$6.00
	Shipping	$2.00
	Duties	$0.50
Landed Cost		$8.50
Amazon Fees	Fulfillment Fee	$3.00
	Referral Fee	$4.00
Net Profit Before Advertising		**$12.50**
Margin		**44.64%**
Return on Investment		**147.06%**

Fails The Test: Beauty Blender

Page one results for this product are selling for an average of $9. I could source the average 5piece set for around $1.50 with a quick search on Alibaba. With those numbers, I will only see around a 30% profit margin. Though it's not *terrible*, it does not surpass our 45% target. So this product will be a pass.

Revenue	Price	$9.00
	COGS	$1.50
	Shipping	$0.50
	Duties	$0.10
Landed Cost		$2.10
Amazon Fees	Fulfillment Fee	$3.50
	Referral Fee	$0.75
Net Profit Before Advertising		**$2.65**
Margin		**29.44%**
Return on Investment		**126.19%**

Criteria #4: Long-Term — It's Not A Trend Or Fad.

General rule of thumb: If you want to make money all year round (which should be your goal), it's very important to stay away from sales spikes. This means no seasonal products or fad products that have suddenly gained a lot of popularity.

Passes The Test: Wall Clock

Though it has seen its ups and downs, a product like a wall clock does not depend on the season to get sales. It's also something that has been around for a long time and will continue to be. Market Intelligence proves this with its consistent sales trend chart, and Google Trends backs it up looking back through 2004 search history.

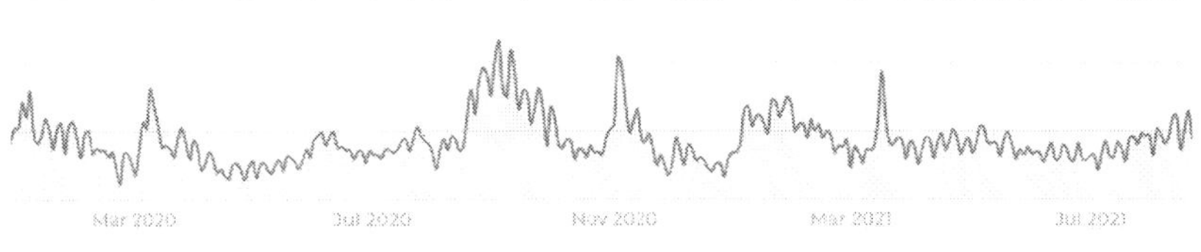

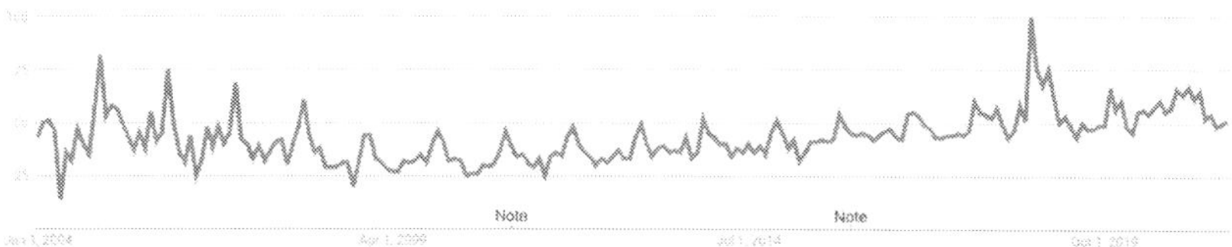

Fails The Test: Sunset Lamp

Here we see a very sudden rise in searches for sunset lamps. Similar to fidget spinners, this product is getting a lot of interest in a short amount of time, which may seem like the perfect opportunity to make a lot of money. However, if you jump in at the peak, you're destined to lose. That's exactly what happened for me with another trend product—silicone makeup sponges. This product is a no-no, even though Viral Launch gives a product idea score of 4.5 out of 5.

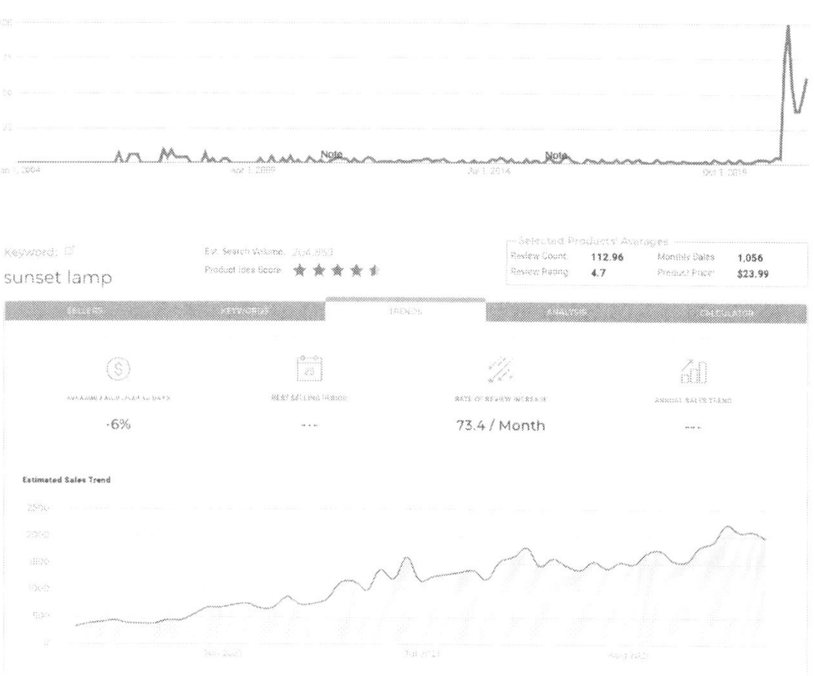

To recap, you're looking for a product that satisfies all of these criteria. And keep in mind, lots of people are reading this book. It may be best to stay away from the product ideas we've just gone through.

Criteria	Description	General Rule Of Thumb
High demand	There are already people searching for and buying it.	Search volume: Above 5,000 BSR: 3 Products below 20,000
Low competition	Top-selling products don't have a ton of reviews.	Reviews: Below 300
Profitable	It fits your budget and makes money after expenses.	Budget: Spend ½ on product costs Margin: Above 35%
Long-Term	It's not a trend or fad.	No sales spikes

> Pro Tip:
>
> Do not launch a me-too product.

There are far too many of those on Amazon. Think from a shopper's perspective, and understand that people shop based on emotion. As you're doing product research, consider a product that you're a user of. That way, you can innovate on the product instead of relying on a price war to win sales.

Step 2: Source Your Product

Once you are confident in which product you want to launch, it's time to get it manufactured and shipped to Amazon. While that may sound a bit daunting, there is a proven roadmap to getting this done right.

At a high level, you need to:

A. Reach out to suppliers
B. Negotiate your price
C. Order and evaluate product samples
D. Set up a Seller Central account
E. Get your barcode
F. Pay for your first batch of inventory
G. Ship the products into Amazon

Let's go through each one so that you know exactly how to move forward.

Reach Out To Suppliers

First, you'll want to head to Alibaba.com. This website lets you find manufacturers who will produce your branded product in bulk. Typically, these suppliers are overseas.

To begin, select Suppliers from the top dropdown and search for your selected product.

Scroll through the suppliers, and you'll see that some are identified as Gold Suppliers with Trade Assurance. These badges are ideal but not necessary. Start clicking into suppliers' pages and looking through their photos and other products to see if they appear legit.

> **Action Step:**
>
> Add at least 50 suppliers to your Favorites by clicking the Star on those that look like they might be a good option. You will need to create an Alibaba account to do this.

From your list of favorites, you can select all 50+ suppliers, add them to a Group, and send that Group a mass email.

When you send this initial email, you're seeking a quote for 2 months worth of inventory (you can use Market Intelligence to get an idea of how much you'll sell in one month on page one... and double it).

> **Action Step:**
>
> Send a mass email that includes:
>
> - The number of pieces you want
> - The name of the product
> - A photo of the product
> - Exact specifications based on reviews of top products (no chemical smell, 2 sizes, etc.)

- A request for EXW and FOB pricing
- A sense of urgency
- A signoff from you (you may call yourself a Senior Sourcing Agent for legitimacy)

Negotiate Your Price

Your next step is to organize the quotes you receive into a folder or a spreadsheet. For suppliers that responded clearly and in a timely manner, it's time to negotiate on pricing. The first step is to let them know that the price is too high, and from there you'll be able to find middle ground. Here are a few tips for negotiating:

- Tip #1: Search for your product on 1688.com in Mandarin using Google Translate and compare the quotes there for leverage.
- Tip #2: Photoshop the price of another quote, blur out the name of the supplier, and send it back to see if they'll drop their price.

Order And Evaluate Samples

By now, you should have 1-3 favorite suppliers who have shown they can be helpful. Now it is time to order samples directly to your home from these top suppliers. Simply send them a message letting them know what you're looking for in samples, and they'll arrange it.

Typically samples range from $50 to $60. They will likely be shipped by air and can typically be paid for via PayPal. Make sure you ask your supplier if they can deduct the sample cost from your future, larger order. Most suppliers will agree to do so.

When you get your samples, use them and evaluate them. Even order your top competitors' products on Amazon to compare. Now is the time to provide feedback you may have to your supplier to set yourself up for differentiation in the market, good reviews, and profitable sales.

Set Up A Seller Central Account

Setting up your Amazon Seller Central account the right way is really important so that you don't get suspended before you even start selling.

Go to sellercentral.amazon.com/ and click Start Selling.

Here's what you need to set up an Amazon Seller Central account:

- Email: Should be created just for your business (use GSuite)
- Name: Your legal name or your business name
- Address: Business address (home address is okay)
- Deposit Method: OFX or other bank details for Amazon to send money to
- Charge Method: Credit card info for your monthly Amazon account fee
- Documentation: Prove who you are with utility bills, credit card bills, etc.
- (US Only) Federal Tax ID: Social Security Number
- Business Number: Incorporation number if you have one

When you are prompted to, "Tell us about your products," check yes on all boxes (you have a UPC... even if you don't yet, you own a brand, you'd like to target business buyers, etc.)

It will also ask you for your Unique Business Display Name, which will be your storefront name. This does not have to be your actual business name and should not be something that is trademarked.

There are two different types of Amazon Seller Plans:

1. Individual: Pay a per-item fee of $0.99 USD plus applicable referral fees
2. Professional: $39.99 USD/month or $29.99 CAD

We recommend you start with the Professional Plan. This won't break the bank and gives you no inventory limit.

Pay close attention when you get to the Identity Verification section.

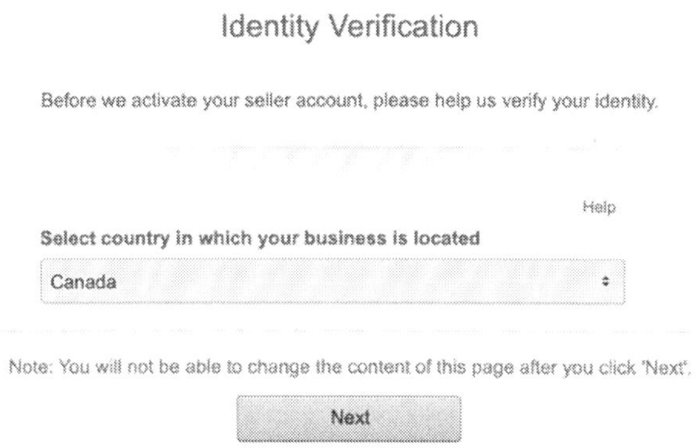

Identity Verification

Before we activate your seller account, please help us verify your identity.

Help

Select country in which your business is located

Canada

Note: You will not be able to change the content of this page after you click 'Next'.

Next

It will ask you for your passport or driver's license information along with your business address. Please make sure your name and business address match *exactly* what you've inputted in earlier stages.

As long as you do this, they should approve your account within a few days!

Get Your Barcode

In order to sell a product on Amazon, you need an FNSKU (Fulfillment Network Stock Keeping Unit) placed on every single item. This is a barcode that Amazon uses to track products in their warehouses.

The first step to getting an FNSKU from Amazon is to purchase a UPC (Universal Product Code). One UPC can be purchased for $30 from GS1, or you can purchase them in bulk. Please make sure to buy a brand new UPC from GS1 and not a second-hand one from a reseller, so that you're setting yourself up for long-term success.

> **Get Your U.P.C. Barcodes from GS1 US**
>
> Whether you're selling in stores, online, or both, the right place to turn for barcodes is GS1 US.

Your UPC will activate in 48-72 hours, and from there you can create your Amazon listing. Here are the steps to turn your UPC into your Amazon barcode (FNSKU):

1. Under *Catalog*, click *Add Products* and then *I'm adding a product not sold on Amazon*
2. Search your product and select your ideal category
3. Complete the *Vital Info* tab with your UPC code as well as the *Offer* tab then click *Save*
4. After 15 minutes, under the *Inventory* tab, click *Manage Inventory* and then *Edit*
5. Upload at least one image and fill in a very simple description, then click *Save*
6. After 15 minutes, find *Change to Fulfilled by Amazon* under the dropdown next to *Save*

7. Under *Barcode Type* select *Amazon barcode* and then hit *Convert only*
8. Complete the following questions and then click *Save and Continue*
9. After 15 minutes, you'll see an FNSKU in your Inventory tab to the left of the Edit button

Congrats! Now you have an FNSKU. You can now ask your manufacturer to print the barcode directly on your products/packaging.

Pay For Your First Batch Of Inventory

Now your product is ready to order. Congratulations! Your next step is to send a purchase order to your supplier, put down a 30% deposit, and schedule an inspection.
What Should My Purchase Order Include?

- Issuer (you) and issue date
- Manufacturer's name, address, point of contact, and phone number
- Product name and specifications
- Quantity
- Unit price and total price
- Payment terms and bank information
- Delivery information
- Terms and conditions including communication, sample fees, inspections, and delays
- Photos of the product and FNSKU

(BUYER'S COMPANY NAME)

(Buyer's Company Address / Contact Information)

PURCHASE ORDER

P.O. Issuer	P.O. Issued Date	Proforma Invoice No.	P.O. Reference No.
(Buyer's Authorized Issuer)			

SELLER'S NAME		SELLER'S OFFICE ADDRESS	PAYMENT DETAILS	
			Incoterm	Term
			EXW,FOB & Other	30-70 or 25-75
Point of Contact	Telephone	SELLER'S FACTORY ADDRESS	Payment Via	
			TRADE ASSURANCE / EFT See Additional page for details	

ITEM NO.	SUPPLIES / PRODUCT	QUANTITY	UNIT	UNIT PRICE	TOTAL AMOUNT
1	**Product Name:** **Specification:** (Add another page if needed) Material: Product Dimension: Product Weight: Color: Master Carton Dimension: Maser Carton Weight: Individual Box Dimension: Individual Box Weight: Certification if any: HS Code: **Others:** a. Insert Card b. Care Label (If Required) c. Instruction Manual (If Required) ***See attached illustration / photo of product				

Total Amount in Words	Amount in Figures

Payment Instruction
30%/25% to initiate production & the balance payment of 70%/75% or as per agreed by Seller & Buyer

How Do I Place A 30% Deposit?

Your 30% deposit initiates manufacturing, and you'll pay the rest when the manufacturer ships the inventory. There are two common methods of payment. The first is through wire transfer. If you are not using Mercury bank, I recommend OFX, an international money transfer and currency exchange. Makes it super easy.

Or, you can opt for Alibaba Trade Assurance. This is Alibaba's own escrow service, where they'll hold your money for you while the transaction is verified. This is a great option if you want to be extra careful sending money overseas.

How Do I Conduct An Inspection?
Inspection agencies go directly to the factory and ensure your product has been manufactured to your liking. If the inspection passes, great! If it fails, hold your 70% and work with the manufacturer to get it resolved. Contact an inspection company nearby the factory around a week before the inventory is ready to be inspected. I recommend you check out Effition Inspection Agency if available.

Ship Your Products Into Amazon's Warehouse

Congratulations! You have successfully placed your order. Many, many people do not make it to this point. So, take a moment and give yourself a pat on the back.

Alright, there is plenty of work still left to be done. Next you'll want to create a shipment plan in Amazon's Seller Central. You can do this by going to *Manage Inventory* ⇢ *Send/Replenish Inventory.*

You've got case-packed products, and you'll want to communicate with your manufacturer to determine how many cases you have. Likely the merchant (your manufacturer) will prep and label the products, but confirm with them. Once your shipment is created, give the labels to your manufacturer to print and place on the shipment.

Packing type What's this?

When your suppliers are packing up your products and getting them ready to ship to Amazon, you need to tell them about the Amazon Prep Requirements. This is because inventory that arrives at a fulfillment center without proper preparation or labeling may incur a preparation fee.

Just as an example, when your supplier packs up your products into 1 case, the case pack limit is 150 units per case. So if you are ordering 1500 units for your first patch of inventory, then you would need 10 cases x 150 units in each case.

Now your order will be on its way soon! Here's what to expect during this time:

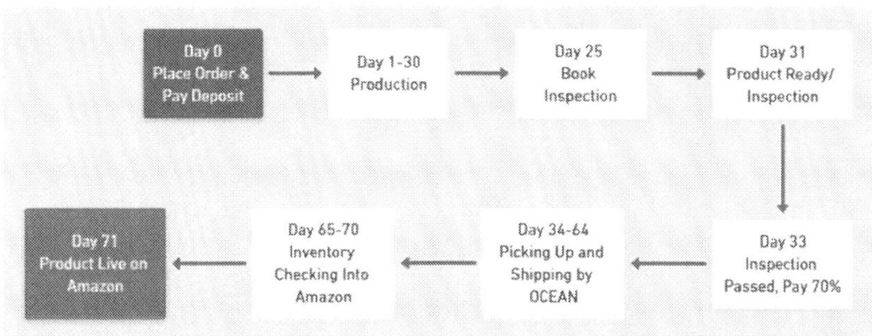

Step 3: Launch On Amazon

While you are waiting for your inventory to arrive at Amazon, there is plenty you can do to prepare. The launching process is incredibly important. You cannot expect shoppers to flock to your product just because it is live. So, spend some time here. Make all of your effort up until this point worth it.

Prepare Your Listing

There are two important components of your listing that you need to develop before your product arrives: photos and copy. And the number one mistake I see my students make is not putting in enough effort to showcase quality.

So, let's start with photos. Take a look at your competitors to see what's working for them and how you can stand out. And read popular reviews on existing products to find what features people are looking for, so that you can showcase those in your images.

Here are the types of images to consider including on your listing:

1. Product photos: Professional studio images with white background
2. Lifestyle photos: Images that show the product in-use and in-context
3. Infographic: Cross-breed of text with photography to showcase benefits
4. 3D render: Animated image on a computer

Make a list for your photographer of exactly what you want to showcase in the images. And yes—that means you need to hire a professional photographer. Don't skimp and use your iPhone here. This really matters for your conversion rate and ultimately your bank account.

Here are some great photos I received after giving very specific instructions to my photographer:

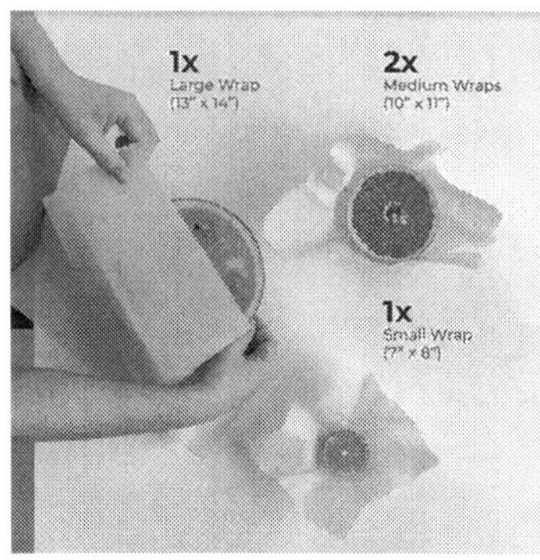

By the way, if you like the images above, check out: https://www.amz.photography/.

Now let's talk about your listing's copy. These are the actual words that compose the page. This is truly an art and a science.

It's an art because shoppers will read the words and be convinced (or not convinced) to purchase your product.

It's a science because Amazon's algorithm reads the listing to determine what your product actually is—and it uses this information to determine where and how often to show your products to shoppers. Basically... the stronger your copy, the better your sales.

Therefore, it's VERY important that you place the right keywords or phrases in your listing in the right placement. Amazon considers some sections of your listing are more important than others. So your most important keywords will go in your title, while less important words can be saved for the bullet points and description.

Your first step is to find the most important keywords to include in your listing so that shoppers can find your product. Head to Viral Launch's tool called Keyword Research, and type in your product.

Inside, you will see the volume estimates, which denotes how many people are searching for those terms every month. If you click *Create Listing*, it'll take you to a Listing Builder where you can make sure you're including every single important keyword so that you don't miss a relevant shopper.

Don't be afraid to fill your title with keywords, even if it's really long. Your title is the most important real estate on Amazon, which is why you will often see long titles. And don't forget... you still need to sell your product to humans! Add words between keywords that make it readable and compelling to shoppers.

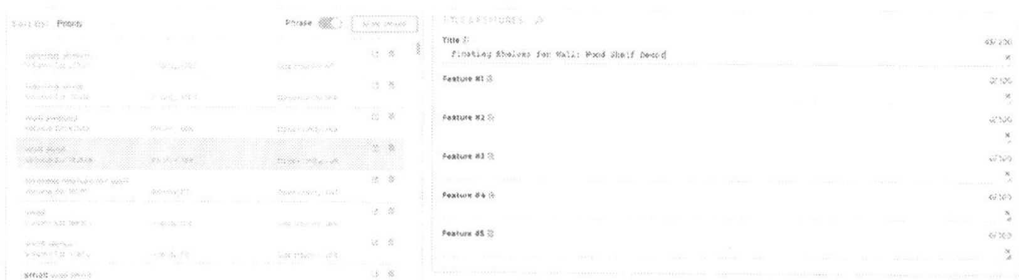

Once your copy is created, take it into Seller Central and paste it into the corresponding fields under Inventory > Manage Inventory > Edit.

> **Pro Tip:**
>
> I came across a really cool software tool that will actually write your product description for you. It's called conversion.ai, and there is a 7-day free trial.

Head to the Amazon product description section, and enter the information it asks for. You can use a competitor's bullets as a starting point for the "Tell us about your product" field. Choose a tone of voice from their options, such as "casual feminine" (depending on your target market), and the tool will literally create your copy for you! It's almost always 1,000 times better than what I could create.

You can do the same thing for Amazon product features.

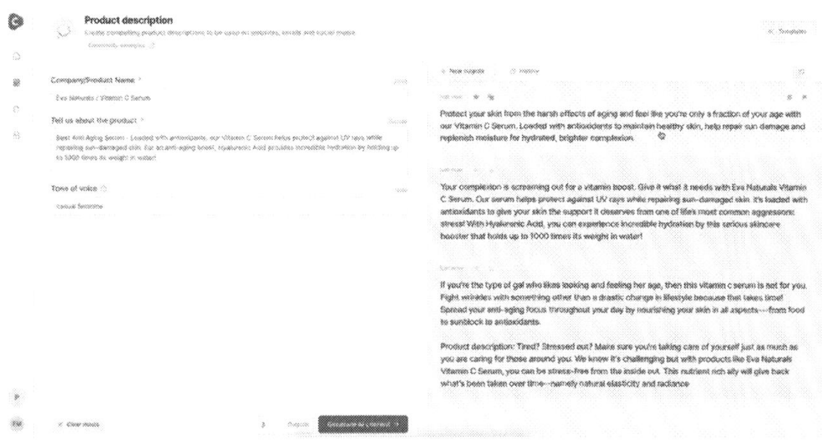

Gather Reviews

The number of reviews you have, along with your actual star rating, is really important for driving both clicks and sales. However, gathering reviews on Amazon is notoriously difficult.

The first thing you need to do is read Amazon's review policy. There are some "white-hat" (aka by the book) and "grey-hat" (aka technically against the rules) techniques that we will cover in this section, so know the rules and use your best judgment based on your risk tolerance.

Here is Amazon's outlined review policy:

Customer product reviews policies

Customer reviews are an integral part of the customer shopping experience on Amazon. Customers use these reviews to learn more about the product, assess whether it fits their needs, and make an informed purchase decision. Customer reviews also help sellers understand the customers' sentiment about their products, what features or aspects of the product customers like, and what areas need improvements. Reviews also provide sellers with ideas on how to improve their products. In order for customer reviews to continue to provide these benefits to customers and sellers, they have to remain a true and authentic reflection of customers' experiences with the products.

Amazon's Community Guidelines have specific policies that are meant to protect the authenticity of Customer Reviews, and we ask you to comply with these policies and report any violations you might notice.

We strongly urge you to thoroughly review Amazon Customer Reviews policies and immediately correct any violating actions. It is important that you educate your business partners, employees, and any third-party partners you work with about these policies as well. Any infractions by your business partners, employees, or third party agencies will result in enforcement actions, even if it happened without your knowledge or consent.

Violations to Customer Reviews policies include, but are not limited to, these actions:

- A seller posts a review of their own product or their competitor's product.
- A seller offers a third party a financial reward, discount, free products, or other compensation in exchange for a review on their product or their competitor's product. This includes using services that sell customer reviews, websites, or social media groups.
- A seller offers to provide a refund or reimbursement after the buyer writes a review (including reimbursement via a non-Amazon payment method). This could be done via buyer-seller messaging on Amazon or directly contacting customers or using 3rd party services, websites, or social media groups.
- A seller uses a third-party service that offers free or discounted products tied to a review (for example, a review club that requires customers to register their Amazon public profile so that sellers can monitor their reviews).
- A family member or employee of the seller posts a review of the seller's product or a competitor's product.
- A seller asks a reviewer to change or remove their review. They might also offer a refund or other compensation to a reviewer in exchange for doing so.
- A seller diverts negative reviews to be sent to them or to a different feedback mechanism while positive reviews are sent to Amazon.
- A seller creates a variation relationship between products with the aim of manipulating reviews and boosting a product's star rating via review aggregation.
- A seller inserts a request for a positive Amazon review or an incentive in exchange for a review into product packaging or shipping box.
- A seller uses a customer account to write or change a review on his or his competitor's product.

And here's what they have to say about their zero-tolerance policy:

Amazon has a zero-tolerance policy towards any customer reviews violations. If we detect any attempts to manipulate customer reviews, we take immediate actions that include, but are not limited to:

- Immediate and permanent withdrawal of the seller's selling privileges on Amazon and withholding of funds.
- The removal of all the product's reviews and preventing the product from receiving future reviews or ratings.
- Permanent delisting of the product from Amazon.
- Legal action against the seller, including lawsuits and referral to civil and criminal enforcement authorities.
- Disclosing the seller's name and other related information publicly.

Now that you know what's expected, I will walk you through how many sellers go about gathering those coveted reviews. Many sellers do opt for the grey-hat techniques, but again, you will need to use your best judgment here.

- **(Grey Hat) Friends And Family:** Ask people outside of your immediate household to purchase your product and leave a review.
- **(White Hat) Viral Launch Extension:** With the click of a button, you can request a review from everyone who has already purchased your product
- **(White Hat) Insert Cards:** In your product packaging, you can include a physical insert card that asks for a review. Just be sure it's neutral language and doesn't ask specifically for a "positive" review.
- **(White Hat) Feedback Whiz:** Use this email software to follow up with customers after they receive their product to neutrally ask for a review. This is a good long-term strategy.

Start Advertising On Amazon

Here's a mind-blowing stat: 80% of all clicks on Amazon are on the first page. So if you've just launched your product and it's sitting on page 10 or page 100 for all major keywords, how are you supposed to make sales?

PPC (or pay-per-click advertising) is the best way to blast through all that noise and sell directly to your customer. And remember, this is a pay-to-play game. You're competing for sales with other sellers in your niche using a bid and a budget. You must spend money to make money here.

In general, it's a great way to drive sales through your listing and gain traction in the marketplace.

PPC Overview

Your main goal should be to target every single possible keyword and product detail page available. And as we're setting our bids (the amount we are willing to pay for a click), the goal is to continually test it until we find what is profitable.

To accomplish this, we first need to discover keywords and product targets and then bid on them. As we adjust our bids, we will eventually find the sweet spot.

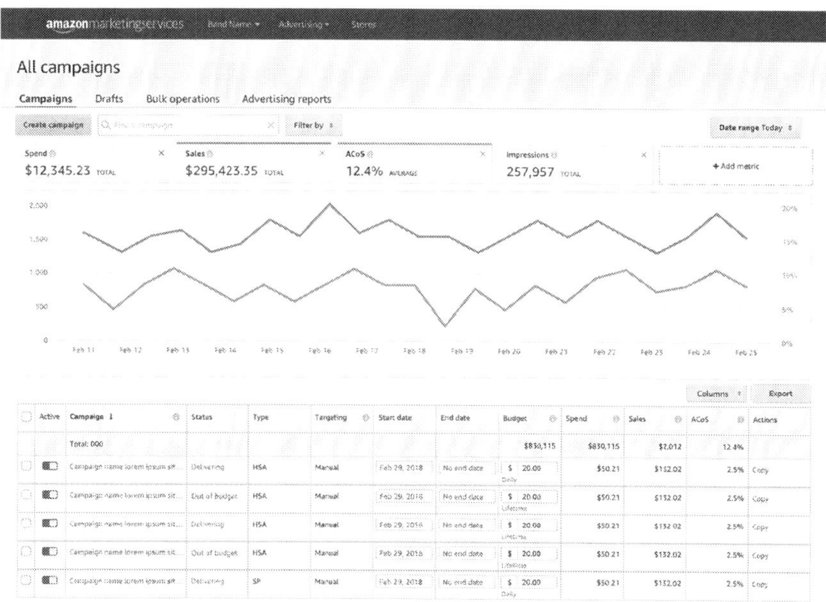

General Strategy

- Launch campaigns to discover keywords and product targets
- Extract keywords to target them
- Extract ASINs (Amazon Standard Identification Numbers) to target them
- Optimize bids regularly
- Test new strategies
- Refresh old keywords
- Launch aggressively for rank—then optimize for profit

Finally, let's go over the two different types of PPC campaigns.

Auto Campaigns are used to "mine" relevant keywords or products that your customer is searching for. Use these keywords or products to create manual campaigns and get more targeted. These are the easiest campaigns to create, but they cannot be optimized.

Manual Campaigns are created from scratch. You choose your own keywords and bid on which ones you think shoppers will purchase through. This method is more hands-on, but you can optimize much further.

Start running PPC as you're receiving your first reviews to gather data, and optimize as you go.

Run Influencer Marketing Campaigns

As more people start selling on Amazon, it's really important to build a real brand. Doing so requires more than just relying on Amazon to provide you with shoppers and customers.

One method that worked really well for us when building Sdara Skincare was Influencer Marketing. So let's pull back the curtain so that you can copy our strategy and implement it in your own business.

What Is Influencer Marketing?

Influencer marketing is a type of social media marketing that uses endorsements and product mentions from influencers. The top 3 goals:

1. Increase brand awareness
2. Reach new audiences
3. Sell and convert more

There are countless channels you can use to find influencers and promote your products... Instagram, YouTube, Twitter, Google, TikTok, Facebook, and so on.

So how do you get started? Your first step is to define your ABCs:

A. Audience: Who is your demographic? How old are they? What are they interested in?

B. Budget: Whether you have $10 or $10,000, there are plenty of influencers.

C. Channel: Where do your ideal customers spend the most time? Instagram? Facebook?

Defining these key elements will help you find the right influencers who will ultimately convert the best for your products.

Here's an example of a post that was successful for Sdara from an influencer, @karinium

And here is another influencer post, this time for my friend Selene's company. She built Vitae Apparel, an activewear brand, solely based on influencer marketing.

Build Your Social Media

After defining your ABCs, this is the first step to success. When you're seeking out influencers, they are going to visit your social media page to check out who you are and what you're promoting.

If you don't have a good social media presence for your brand, they're probably not going to work with you. At the end of the day, they're putting their name and their fame behind a product when promoting it.

There are three pillars to your social presence: Your profile, content, and interactions.

PROFILE

Your profile needs to have an aesthetically pleasing brand identity. This includes a simple username, your logo, and a consistent color theme. Your About section should be short and sweet and communicate exactly what your brand does. Make sure to include contact information and your website or a Linktree.

CONTENT

There are really four types of content you can and should post:

1. Educate people on the product or industry

2. Highlight your customers (ask for poster's permission)

3. Interact with the community

4. Entertain your followers

When it comes to content, the more the better. Here is the suggested posting frequency:

- Images: 5+ per week (use Unsplash.com for royalty-free images)
- Videos: 1+ per week
- Stories: 1+ per day

INTERACTIONS

Interacting with your community helps your followers and customers understand that there is actually a human being behind the screen. Like and respond to comments on your post with thoughtful and engaging words. And have fun with it! Repost when customers tag you, use relevant hashtags, and overall interact with those who are showing your brand love.

Set Goals And Find Influencers

There are literally millions of "influencers" in the world. And not every single one is the right one for you to work with. So how should you go about finding influencers that mesh well with your brand and ultimately make you money?

DETERMINE CAMPAIGN GOALS

Why are you launching this campaign? Answering this question will help you understand which type of campaign you want to run. Are you running a giveaway? Is this a product launch? Is it a long-term or short-term collaboration?

DEFINE YOUR CAMPAIGN AUDIENCE

- Who are your customers? Example: 25-40-year-old females, moms, teachers, family members of moms, friends of moms
- What is your target location? Example: United States only
- Where does your audience interact? Example: New moms use YouTube for tutorial videos, hacks, and reviews

SET YOUR BUDGET

How much you have to spend will ultimately determine the size and number of influencers that you can work with at any given time. You will most likely deal with micro-influencers, middle-influencers, and macro-influencers.

- $50-$500 per post: Micro-influencers (10K-250K followers)
- $500-$1,000 per post: Middle-influencers (250K-500K followers)
- $1,000-$4,000 per post: Macro-influencers (500K-1M followers)
- $5,000+ per post: Celebrities (1M+ followers)

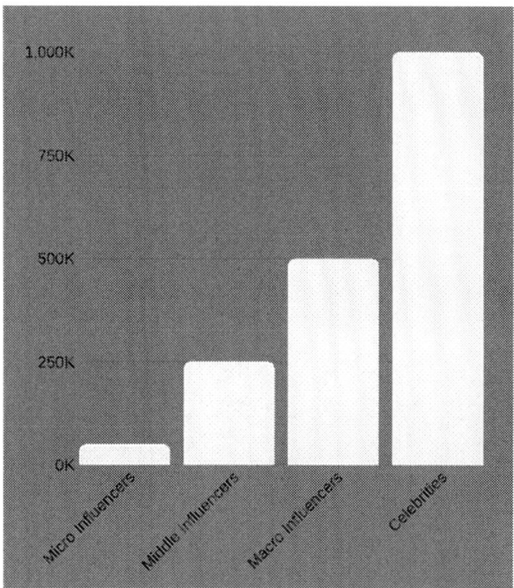

When you are reviewing an influencer's page and gathering a list of influencers you might want to work with, it's important to ask yourself the following questions:

- Does this influencer and their lifestyle fit my brand image?
- Have they worked with any of my competitors?
- Who is this influencer's current audience?
- Is my target audience active on the platform or channel primarily used by this influencer?
- Does working with this influencer make sense for my budget?
- Has this influencer actually used any of my products?

- Are they already a customer?
- Does this person have a personality I want to work with?
- What will this influencer expect from me?

Before you pay an influencer any money and as you're communicating with them about a potential collaboration, you can ask them for their metrics. Sites like Instagram and YouTube provide influencers with a lot of data on their account, and seeing these metrics will help you make an informed decision about the questions above.

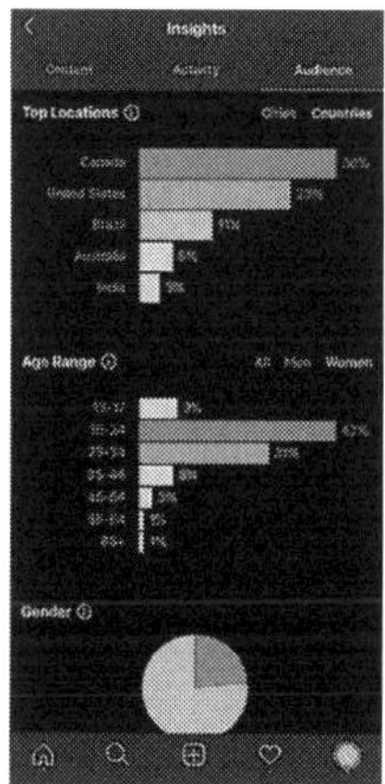

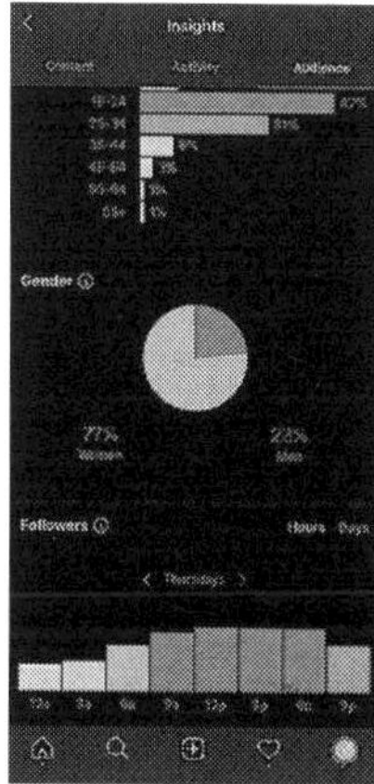

Here's a template you can use to reach out to brands. It's just an example, and keep in mind that adding a personal touch can go a long way.

Hi ______,

I hope you're doing well :). My name is _____ and I'm the Influencer Manager here at _____. I just wanted to stop by and let you know that I absolutely love your page and the content you create!

I'd love to send out some of our products for you to try out, with no obligations and if you genuinely love the products we'd love to hear from you!

If you're interested in trying out some of our collection, please respond with the best mailing address and I'll get a package sent out.

Have a lovely evening!

Best,

______

Run Your Campaign

As the owner of your brand, it's your job to give influencers the right tools and information so that they know what to say about the product.

Providing a brand kit, mood board, and photo guidelines is a great way to set up your influencer campaigns for success because the poster has context on what they should be posting, what works, and why.

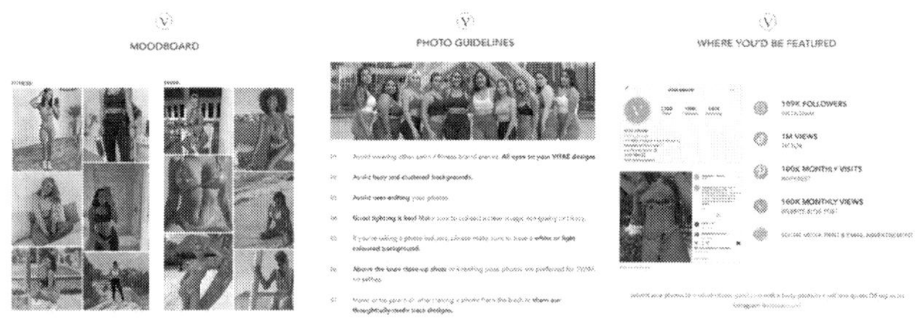

COMPENSATION

There is no one right way to pay influencers. Everything is really customizable between the influencer you're working with and your brand. Choosing which direction to go depends on what your budget is and how willing the influencer is to work with you. That said, here are some common ways to compensate:

- Sponsored posts
- Sponsored stories

- Sponsored giveaways
- Paid content creation
- Commission on sales
- Monthly payments
- Free store gift card
- Extra free product
- Monthly collaborations
- Extra commissions

However you choose to compensate, once you start paying people, it's important to outline expectations in writing. This should include things like services provided, the terms of the agreement, expected performance, compensation, and confidentiality.

Here's an example that you can customize for your own brand:

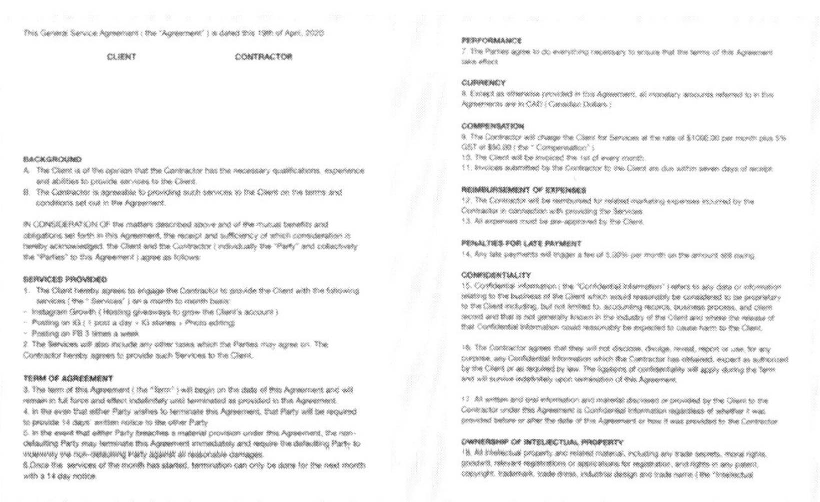

This General Service Agreement (the "Agreement") is dated this 19th of April, 2020

CLIENT | CONTRACTOR

BACKGROUND

A. The Client is of the opinion that the Contractor has the necessary qualifications, experience and abilities to provide services to the Client.

B. The Contractor is agreeable to providing such services to the Client on the terms and conditions set out in the Agreement.

IN CONSIDERATION OF the matters described above and of the mutual benefits and obligations set forth in this Agreement, the receipt and sufficiency of which consideration is hereby acknowledged, the Client and the Contractor (individually the "Party" and collectively the "Parties" to this Agreement) agree as follows:

SERVICES PROVIDED

1. The Client hereby agrees to engage the Contractor to provide the Client with the following services (the " Services") on a month to month basis:
- Instagram Growth (Hosting giveaways to grow the Client's account)
- Posting on IG (1 post a day + IG stories + Photo editing
- Posting on FB 3 times a week

2. The Services will also include any other tasks which the Parties may agree on. The Contractor hereby agrees to provide such Services to the Client.

TERM OF AGREEMENT

3. The term of this Agreement (the "Term") will begin on the date of this Agreement and will remain in full force and effect indefinitely until terminated as provided in this Agreement.
4. In the even that either Party wishes to terminate this Agreement, that Party will be required to provide 14 days' written notice to the other Party.
5. In the event that either Party breaches a material provision under this Agreement, the non-defaulting Party may terminate this Agreement immediately and require the defaulting Party to indemnify the non-defaulting Party against all reasonable damages.
6. Once the services of the month has started, termination can only be done for the next month with a 14 day notice.

PERFORMANCE

7. The Parties agree to do everything necessary to ensure that the terms of this Agreement take effect.

CURRENCY

8. Except as otherwise provided in this Agreement, all monetary amounts referred to in this Agreements are in CAD (Canadian Dollars)

COMPENSATION

9. The Contractor will charge the Client for Services at the rate of $[illegible] per month plus 5% GST of $[illegible] (the " Compensation")
10. The Client will be invoiced the 1st of every month.
11. Invoices submitted by the Contractor to the Client are due within seven days of receipt.

REIMBURSEMENT OF EXPENSES

12. The Contractor will be reimbursed for related marketing expenses incurred by the Contractor in connection with providing the Services.
13. All expenses must be pre-approved by the Client.

PENALTIES FOR LATE PAYMENT

14. Any late payments will trigger a fee of [illegible]% per month on the amount still owing.

CONFIDENTIALITY

15. Confidential information (the "Confidential Information") refers to any data or information relating to the business of the Client which would reasonably be considered to be proprietary to the Client including, but not limited to, accounting records, business process, and client record and that is not generally known in the industry of the Client and where the release of that Confidential Information could reasonably be expected to cause harm to the Client.

16. The Contractor agrees that they will not disclose, divulge, reveal, report or use, for any purpose, any Confidential Information which the Contractor has obtained, except as authorized by the Client or as required by law. The obligations of confidentiality will apply during the Term and will survive indefinitely upon termination of this Agreement.

17. All written and oral information and material disclosed or provided by the Client to the Contractor under this Agreement is Confidential Information regardless of whether it was provided before or after the date of this Agreement or how it was provided to the Contractor.

OWNERSHIP OF INTELLECTUAL PROPERTY

18. All intellectual property and related material, including any trade secrets, moral rights, goodwill, relevant registrations or applications for registration, and rights in any patent, copyright, trademark, trade dress, industrial design and trade name (the "Intellectual

MEASURE RESULTS

Make sure to keep an eye on how this campaign ultimately affects your brand and your bottom line. Check for engagement, impressions, conversions, new followers, and ultimately your return on investment.

If the influencer is driving traffic directly towards your Amazon listing, I would recommend that the influencer you're working with signs up for the Amazon Affiliate Program.

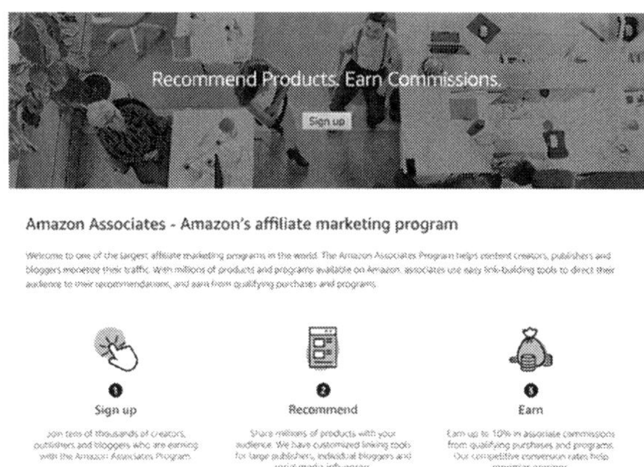

This is one of the largest influencer marketing programs in the world, and it's extremely easy to sign up. So basically, if you give your product to an influencer, they can create a link through this tool to direct traffic to it. From there, Amazon will pay them a percentage of the sale (around 8%) out of Amazon's own pocket.

As the brand, you can offer to match Amazon's commissions. This is a win-win because it's purely performance-driven. When they send a screenshot of their Amazon Affiliate dashboard, then you can send the money.

If the influencer is driving traffic to your website, I recommend using software like Refersion. This will generate a link for them to use that you can track their results through. I highly recommend sending people to Amazon over your website, but know the option is there if you want to try it out in the future.

Finally, it's best to maintain a long-term relationship with any influencer you work with, because the ultimate goal is to have a group of influencers who back you and will work with you on new product launches in the future.

Interested to learn more? Selene Dior, founder of Vitae Apparel, has an agency that manages your Instagram for you. If you're interested in learning more, shoot her an email at dior@vitaeapparel.com.

Step 4: Scale Your Business

Congratulations! If you've made it this far, you have a product live on Amazon that is making sales. The bulk of the work for *this* product is behind you—Woo!

So where do you go from here? I'd recommend the following:

A. Track your progress
B. Optimize your sales
C. Launch more products

Track Your Progress

I teach all of my students to use an FBA Daily Diary. This is a journal where you'll spend 5 minutes per day writing down some statistics about your business.

Doing this provides you with a lot of clarity so that you can make decisions based on data, not emotions. Many people get frustrated because they don't know what's going on with their business.

So fill out this spreadsheet daily:

Launch Date	5/11/2021										
Date (Input Date MMM/DD)	Day	Price $	Review	Session	Conversion (Unit Session) %	Total Unit Sold	Giveaway Unit	PPC	Organic Sale Unit	% of Organic Sale	Change Log
4/27/2021	1		536	0		0	0	0	0		
4/28/2021	2		536	0		0	0	0	0		
4/29/2021	3		536	0		0	0	0	0		
4/30/2021	4		536	0		0	0	0	0		
5/1/2021	5		536	34	17.65%	6	0	3	3	50.00%	
5/2/2021	6		536	21	23.81%	5	0	2	3	60.00%	
5/3/2021	7		536	33	27.27%	9	0	5	4	44.44%	
5/4/2021	8		536	26	30.77%	8	0	6	2	25.00%	
5/5/2021	9		536	45	24.44%	11	0	4	7	63.64%	
5/6/2021	10		536	37	24.32%	9	0	6	3	33.33%	
5/7/2021	11		536	22	50.00%	11	0	9	2	18.18%	
5/8/2021	12		536	32	25.00%	8	0	4	4	50.00%	
5/9/2021	13		536	27	29.63%	8	0	5	3	37.50%	
5/10/2021	14		536	45	20.00%	9	0	4	5	55.56%	
5/11/2021	15	$39.97	536	39	20.51%	8	0	3	5	62.50%	
5/12/2021	16		536	40	35.00%	14	0	6	8	57.14%	
5/13/2021	17		536	46	36.96%	17	0	10	7	41.18%	
5/14/2021	18		536	37	48.65%	18	0	0	18	100.00%	
5/15/2021	19		536	25	44.00%	11	0	3	8	72.73%	
5/16/2021	20		541	34	14.71%	5	0	4	1	20.00%	
5/17/2021	21								0		
5/18/2021	22								0		
5/19/2021	23								0		

Here's a little bit about each column:

- *Price:* What is the current selling price?
- *Reviews:* How many reviews do you have?
- *Sessions:* How many people clicked your listing? Find this in Business Reports under "Detail Page Sales and Traffic by Parent Item" and filter for today (two-day data delay).
- *Conversion (Unit Session %):* What percent of shoppers purchase? This will auto-populate once you enter the next data point, Total Units Sold.
- *Total Units Sold:* How many products sold? Find "Units ordered" in the same place.
- *Giveaway Units:* How many products sold that you gave away using Rank & Bank (if applicable - this is another strategy to launch your product with)?
- *PPC:* How many products sold through ads? Go to Advertising Reports > Campaigns > Select your product and filter for today.
- *Organic Sales Unit:* How many products were purchased without an ad? This will auto-populate after you input previous data points.

- *% of Organic Sale:* What percent of sales were purchased without an ad? This will auto-populate and you want it to be as high as possible so that you're profitable.
- *Change Log:* What did you change? Take a note so that you can attribute performance trends to changes, such as raising your price, switching your main image, adding a video, etc.

The second tab is used to track keyword rank. In Viral Launch's Competitor Intelligence, you can see when your page rank changes. Feel free to take a screenshot each day and save it. This way, you can cross-reference both tabs to see what changes are taking place in your business and why.

Optimize Your Sales

It's not enough to throw your product up on Amazon and cross your fingers. Hopefully by this point you've started your PPC ads and have potentially run Rank & Bank.

Reordering products from your manufacturer should be quite straightforward. Learning the balance between positive cash flow and keeping inventory in stock is an important one. You'll need to reorder when you have about a month's worth of inventory left, so that by the time your products arrive at Amazon, your supply is just low enough.

From there... Keep optimizing!

Split test your images, seek out reviews, tighten your ads, and focus on ranking on page one for as many keywords as possible. As your visibility and quality increase, so will your revenue. Keep at it, and do not give up.

One important thing to remember... pivoting isn't necessarily a bad thing. When things aren't working, you've got to remain fluid.

So, what happens if the competition is extremely strong? Or if you aren't making any margin? Or if you're spending tons of money and you cannot seem to stick on page one?

1. Compare product against competitors
2. Start adjusting the basics (price, keyword, title, etc.)
3. Relaunch the product to see if you can get momentum
4. Get feedback and ask for help

If you're still not seeing an upward trend after trying everything, it may be time to cut your losses and move on to the next product. Not every product will be a winner, but we can do everything in our power before this point to give ourselves the best opportunity for profit and success.

Launch More Products

Now you know the full process A to Z. The good news is that from here, the best way to make more money is to repeat that exact framework over and over. The more products you have, the more opportunity for shoppers to find you, and the better the chance that you find a home-run product.

The second and third and fourth time around it will only get easier, because you've already done the hard work of learning something entirely new.

One of the easiest ways to scale your business is to launch variations of your current product, especially if it's one that is making good money.

If you're interested in getting help from a community of 6-8-figure Amazon sellers, then you might want to know more about my mentorship program—FBA Masterclass.

As a student of FBA Masterclass, you receive LIVE group coaching every week, plus over 200+ private training videos that walk you through, step-by-step, what to do on every step of your journey—and more.

To schedule a call to talk to my team, visit
www.fbamasterclass.io/consultation

On your call, my team member will tell you everything you need to know before you decide to start selling on Amazon for yourself, and give you a breakdown of what's included in my mentorship program.

By the end of the call, you might choose to join me and my students in my mentorship program. Or you might choose to go it alone. Either way, the call with my team will give you a good step forward.

7

HOW TO GO FROM $0 TO $1M

"That's what really attracted me to Amazon. Just to kind of have that lifestyle of time and money together. And just building something that was important to me."

— Kyle

Kyle was working for a network marketing company before he got started with Amazon. He was struggling on his own for some time when he came across my strategies that changed his business for the better. Now, he's making almost $200,000 a month.

The average person makes about $1,700,000 in their entire lifetime. Which is about $42,000 per year for a 40-year career.

At that rate, you would have to work nearly 24 years of your life to earn $1,000,000. That's probably not what you would have in mind if I said you can earn $1,000,000.

So what if I told you it was possible to make $1,000,000 within 2 years? It might sound a little far-fetched, but I'll break it down for you now.

(Even if you're thinking, "I'm okay if I can just make a 6-figure income," follow along because all the math is the same.)

Let's Break It Down

So in order to make $1,000,000 by selling products on Amazon, first we need to generate about $1,111,080 a year in revenue.

Wait, why $1,111,080? Why not just $1,000,000?

Well, revenue is basically how much money you generate in your store. Revenue doesn't count how much profit you would actually make. You can earn $1,000,000 in revenue but spend $2,000,000 on advertising. You would actually be in the hole for $1,000,000.

Of that $1,111,080, you can probably expect to earn 30% for profit margins (aka $333,324).

But you might be wondering, "If I'm only making $333,324 a year in profit, how does that add up to $1,000,000? Do I have to do this for 3 years?"

Well, you can, but I'm going to show you a different way. As I said, this can be done within 2 years.

You can actually sell your business. There are tons of investors who are keeping an eye on Amazon FBA businesses. These investors buy FBA businesses the same way they would buy real estate.

Meaning, if you build a business that earns $333,324 in profit, investors are willing to buy it for 3x the value, as long as the income is consistent.

That might sound more complicated than it is. Let's break that down:

	Revenue	
Year	$ 1,111,080	
Month	$ 92,590	$ 27,777
Day	$ 3,086	$ 925.8

So to reach $333,324 a year in profit, you will have to earn $925 in profit a day. Earning $925 a day feels easier than earning $1,000,000, right?

We can actually break this down even further to the individual products. An average product might sell for about $20 a unit. If you sell 15 units a day, you earn $300 in revenue.

Product Value	Units Sold	Revenue
$20	15	$300

And if you build up a portfolio of 10 products (which is possible to do within 2 years) you will reach $3,000 a day in revenue.

$20 a product x 15 units x 10 products
= $3,000 in revenue a day

That's basically the same $3,086 you need to reach your goal of $925 in profit. And if you're able to maintain the same $925 a day in profit (or $333,324 a year) for the last 12 months, investors will definitely be interested in buying your business.

The last 12 months of your income is also known as the Trailing Twelve Months. This is something all investors will look for to determine if your business is worth buying.

That's how you're able to work backward from $1,000,000 to see what numbers you need to reach in business.

What If You Have A Different Goal?

You can break down your goals to whatever you want.

Maybe you just want to be able to go on a big family vacation every year without worrying about every penny you spend.

Let's just take a family of 4 as an example.

You have to buy plane tickets which could easily be $500 per person or $2,000 total. A hotel room could cost you $100 a day. If you stay for 10 days that will add up to $1,000.

That's $3,000 just to get to your destination and a place to stay. If you add up everything including food and activities, you could easily spend $5,000 for one trip.

But that shouldn't be a problem at all, right?

Basically, all you need to do is earn $500 a month in profit. You would only need to sell two to three units a day of a $20 product to reach that goal.

Simple.

What about paying off debt? The average person has about $92,727 in debt when you add up all credit card debt, student loans, mortgages, and more.

Could you pay that off within a year?

You can probably do the math at this point. Here's some space to break down your own goals.

	Revenue	
Year		
Month		
Day		

Product Value	Units Sold	# of Products	Revenue

Product Value x Units Sold x # of Products = Revenue

Don't let the numbers intimidate you.

Maybe you have no idea how you can possibly sell that amount of products at this time. And that's okay.

I've already laid out a lot of strategies you can use right away. But I will give you more strategies and resources you can use in the last two chapters of this book.

If you want to chat or receive extra tips for building your business, connect with me on social media. Follow my Instagram @tomdotcom.ig. If you tag me with a picture of you and this book, I'll make sure to reshare your post.

8

NOW IS THE RIGHT TIME

"Believe in the system. It works."

— Chris

Chris worked a normal 9-5 job managing a store. Before Amazon, he was sourcing products and he wanted to brand his own product, but he had little experience with e-commerce. After, he started making $20,000 with just one product.

If you've read until this point and you're excited about the Amazon opportunity, here's why you need to start now.

Right now as you're reading this, there are a few hotshots who are taking the investment world by storm.

They are known as "Amazon aggregators"—which is a fancy name for companies that buy large numbers of Amazon brands.

Recently, they have become one of the hottest segments of the investment world.

Over the past few years, more than 50 aggregators have emerged.

Many of them have successfully pitched investors and raised millions (if not billions) of dollars to purchase small-to-medium-sized businesses that operate on Amazon—just like the kind we've been discussing throughout this book.

In the first half of 2021, here's how much a few of these aggregators have raised:

- Thrasio has raised $1.35 billion (and by the way, Thrasio are the ones who bought my brand Sdara Skincare—they are super professional and I highly recommend working with them).
- Perch has raised $775 million.
- Elevate Brands has raised $315 million.

That is only 3 examples of around 60 that have popped up in the past few years. These companies will take those brands, pump money and expertise into them, and scale the products to new heights.

One aggregator, called Acquco, even committed to giving away $10,000,000 worth of Teslas for referrals.

So is this a fad? Or is it a long-term trend that will benefit Amazon sellers for years to come?

With 2 million small-to-medium-sized sellers profiting over $25 billion in 2020, according to CNBC, it doesn't seem that this growth is going to slow anytime soon. Which means aggregators like Thrasio and Perch will likely continue buying up these smaller brands.

It's similar to how a company like Unilever, one of the world's largest companies, purchases a bunch of other brands to then have an impressive portfolio to dominate the market: Skippy, Vaseline, Lipton, Dove, and Hellmann's, to name a few.

So why should you care?

Well, because when you're building an Amazon business, not only can you earn a good living and have freedom. But you also have the possibility of one day selling your business too—which we call "exiting your business."

So how can you set up your brand to be an ideal target for these aggregator companies?

Here are a few tips:

1. *Revenue distribution:* These businesses look for brands that have multiple winning products, not just one hero SKU that comprises the majority of sales.

2. *Predictable revenue:* Amazon's Subscribe and Save program shows predictable monthly revenue, which is advantageous when selling the business.

3. *Channel distribution:* Work on having an equal distribution of sales from different channels and platforms such as Amazon, Shopify, and Retail. Sure, master Amazon first. But once you get that down, venture out to show it's a real brand.

An Amazon spokesperson was quoted saying, "This is an exciting opportunity for sellers that want liquidity and to exit the business for a new adventure."

If there was ever a perfect time to be building an Amazon business, it's right now.

If you're interested in learning my strategies in more detail, my mentorship program—FBA Masterclass—might be for you.

As a student of FBA Masterclass, you receive LIVE group coaching every week, plus over 200+ private training videos that walk you through, step-by-step, what to do on every step of your journey—and more.

To schedule a call to talk to my team, visit
www.fbamasterclass.io/consultation

On your call, my team member will tell you everything you need to know before you decide to start selling on Amazon for yourself, and give you a breakdown of what's included in my mentorship program.

By the end of the call, you might choose to join me and my students in my mentorship program. Or you might choose to go it alone. Either way, the call with my team will give you a good step forward.

9

THE SIMPLEST WAY TO GET STARTED

"You need to put yourself first this one time and just do it!"

— Mary

Mary was working in the financial industry as a tech consultant. When she went on maternity leave, she discovered my program in November 2020. By July 2021, she was earning $1,000 a day in revenue with just one product.

Starting an Amazon business is not hard to do, but you do need to put in time and energy.

I'm talking about putting in at least 1 hour a day—especially when you first get started. If you can do 2 hours a day, that's even better.

Later, once you've launched a few products and you're kind of used to things, you take your foot off the gas a bit if you want to.

Unfortunately, many people stop themselves before they get started, because they think the entire process is harder than it actually is.

Fear of taking action is what kills a lot of dreams.

It's better to get started today (and make some mistakes) than to be stuck and never get started at all. So if you want to get started selling on Amazon, but there's something holding you back, here's what I recommend you do.

Just sell your first 20 units.

That's it. You're not looking to get rich. You're not even looking to make a profit. What you are doing is getting your feet wet and getting firsthand experience.

Because guess what? If you can do it with 20 units, you can do it again with 500... and again with 5000.

The important part is that you break the barrier that holds most people back from getting started. Take small actions consistently.

And most importantly, remember *why* you got started.

Maybe you want to give more to your family. Or you want to quit your job and be your own boss. Whatever it is, remember why this is important to you.

When I first got started, the truth is I didn't have a dream to make Sdara into a multimillion-dollar brand.

I just wanted to make enough money to make my parents proud. I wanted to make sure my future family was taken care of financially. And all Christina and I wanted back then was to be able to go to Bali once a year for a nice vacation.

Never in a million years did we think, just 3 years later, that all of this and more would come true.

Today, not only do I have a safety net for my family and me, I am also surrounded by other inspiring entrepreneurs. I can play hockey, which was a childhood dream of mine. And I feel like I can really live exactly how I want to—and that's something that is priceless.

Now, I'm not telling you if you start selling on Amazon, you are guaranteed a dream life.

But what I am saying is that if you don't do this... what are the chances you can live the life you want to with your current job, or any other opportunity you have right now?

If you have a better opportunity, that's amazing.

I wish you the best on your journey.

But if you're looking around and you don't have anything better—why not take a closer look at selling a few products on Amazon?

Yeah, it may not be glamorous like being an influencer. It may not make your parents proud like maybe being a doctor would.

But this is a legitimate business.

It is here to stay. And damn, can it give you a lot of freedom and financial stability in life when done properly.

The way I think about it is you have everything to gain—and next to nothing to lose. Wayne Gretzky, who holds 61 NHL records, said it best:

"You miss 100% of the shots you don't take."

So take a shot and just see for yourself if this is right for you or not. That's the easiest way to really find out, and that way you won't have to wonder: "What if...?"

Selling on Amazon is one of the greatest opportunities of our time.

It's not going to be here forever.

In the coming years, I predict that more and more Fortune 500 companies will be coming into this space. That means it's only going to get harder and harder for the little guys like us.

So now is the time.

You're not too late.

If you want more of my help—whether that's for free or you want to pay for coaching directly with me—both are fine.

Here are a few ways that you can learn more about Amazon from me.

Instagram And YouTube

Search "Tom Wang" and you'll get a lot of great strategies on how to get started on your Amazon journey. Or you can use the links below.

YouTube: youtube.com/TomWang
Instagram: instagram.com/tomdotcom.ig
Instagram handle: @tomdotcom.ig

Chat with me there or receive extra tips for building your business. If you tag me with a picture of you and this book, I'll make sure to reshare your post!

How To Find Your First Winning Product

If you're keen on getting started, the first step is to find your first winning product.

You can visit this link to access a great free training that I put together to help you with this step: www.fbamasterclass.io/privatetraining

How To Become A Mentee Of Mine And Access Me, Tom Wang, Directly

If you want to join me and my students in my mentorship program, I don't accept everyone.

You have to go through a qualification call and watch a few training videos to fully understand the business model first.

They will ask you some basic questions to see if there's a fit or not. If there's potential, they will send you a training video walking you through my mentorship program.

That's all for now.

Thank you for reading my first book and I hope I've inspired you in some way. I hope I've shown you a world full of possibilities you can look forward to.

I look forward to hearing about your success!

—Tom

If there's any support or kind words you want to share about this book, please email me and my team. You can reach us at support@fbamasterclass.io.

Would you be willing to help someone if you got nothing in return?

If you found this book helpful and you think it might help someone else as well, here's what to do. As you probably already know, online reviews help us reach more people.

If you want to chat or receive extra tips for building your business, connect with me on social media. Follow my Instagram @tomdotcom.ig. If you tag me with a picture of you and this book, I'll make sure to reshare your post.

Thanks!

Quick Links

To schedule a call with the FBA Masterclass team visit fbamasterclass.io/consultation

Free Training: fbamasterclass.io/privatetraining

YouTube: youtube.com/TomWang
Instagram: instagram.com/tomdotcom.ig
Instagram handle: @tomdotcom.ig

Learn more about Tom: www.tomwang.io

Made in the USA
Columbia, SC
16 May 2023

16823823R00072